D1096260

7

7

UI

39

F

AI

00

THE NEW SPANISH ARCHITECTURE

THE NEW
SPANISH ARCHITECTURE

Anatxu Zabalbeascoa

Introduction by Peter Buchanan

RIZZOLI
NEW YORK

First published in the United States of America
in 1992 by Rizzoli International Publications, Inc.
300 Park Avenue South, New York, NY 10010

Library of Congress Cataloging-in-Publication Data

Zabalbeascoa, Anatxu.
    The new Spanish architecture / Anatxu Zabalbeascoa;
introduction by Peter Buchanan.
        p.   cm.
    Includes bibliographical references.
    ISBN 0-8478-1532-3   — ISBN 0-8478-1533-1 (pbk.)
    1. Architecture, Modern—20th century—Spain.
    2. Architecture—Spain.   I. Title

NA1308.Z33   1922
720'.946'0904—dc20   92-2835
                                               CIP

Series Designer: Paul Chevannes
Designer: Mary McBride

Printed and bound in Singapore

Front cover photograph: Alberto Campo Baeza, Gaspar house,
  Cádiz, 1991
Front cover drawing: Santiago Calatrava, transversal section,
  Bilbao Airport, Bilbao, 1990–(under construction)
Frontispiece: Enric Batlle & Joan Roig, Fontes Palace,
  Murcia, 1991
Back cover (hardcover only): José Antonio Martínez Lapeña &
  Elías Torres, house in Cap Martinet, Ibiza, 1987

Illustration Credits

For Pablo Zabalbeascoa and Sahara Conca

Acknowledgments

I would like to thank the following individuals and institutions for their help and support in producing this book: John Zukowsky, Curator, and Pauline Saliga, Associate Curator, Department of Architecture of The Art Institute of Chicago, for their trust, and for giving me the opportunity to work with them on several architecture projects; Peter Buchanan, architecture critic and senior editor of the *Architectural Review*, for his introduction to this publication; Pilar Corredoira, for her insights on Galician architecture; Gabriel Coll of the Zazurca studio; Isabel Carull of the Arribas studio; Belén Hermida and Luis Rojo of the Moneo studio; Joan Callis of the Miralles studio; Anthony Tishausser of the Calatrava-Zurich studio; and Josep Rigol of the Lluis Casals photography studio, for their interest, patience, and help. I am also grateful to Pedro Carretero for his views on Majorca's architecture; to Berta Antich, Coordinator of the Centro de Documentación of the Escuela Elisava in Barcelona; to the library staff of COAC, the architecture association of Catalonia, and to the generous photographers whose works illustrate this book: Paolo Roselli, Hisao Suzuki, Lluis Casals, Xavier Basiana, Jordi Sarrá, and Mónica Roselló, for their photographs, time, and professionalism. I also thank Miguel Ruano for his time, support, advice, editing, patience, and for granting me access to his books, files, and architectural periodicals, which have greatly helped me in my work. Finally, my recognition and gratitude are due to all the architects whose work is featured here.

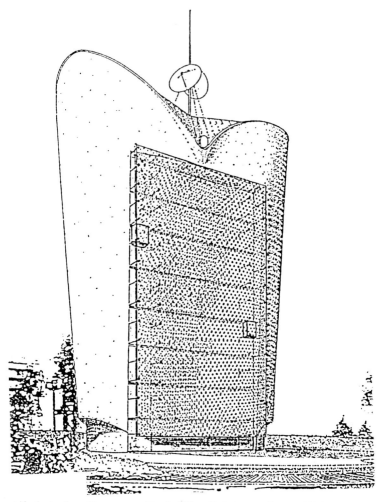

Alfredo Arribas, Marugame office building, Takamatsu, Japan, 1991–

Contents

INTRODUCTION

Peter Buchanan

ALL ARCHITECTS' eyes are on Spain. Yet this is not just because the Seville Expo 92 and Barcelona Olympics are graced by high profile buildings by international stars. Just as staging the Olympics is only the climax to Barcelona's extraordinary feat of self-transformation, so what is really remarkable is the profusion of very fine new work by local architects and how these contribute to this larger whole. Each such building, plaza, or park is much more sensitive to local context, history, and aspirations than the works of the international stars—and often enough superior in every other way too.

In the early eighties architectural works from the initial phases of Barcelona's transformation were the first to draw international attention to the effloresence of talent precipitated by Spain's return to democracy. Crucial to this flowering were both the evaporation of the restrictive atmosphere of the Franco period and then the creative collusion of left-wing politicians with avant-garde architects and artists, all determined to build anew Spain's rundown public realm and culture. But it would

not have bloomed in such a variety of design approaches and quantity and quality of built works without secure roots in the past.

As Anatxu Zabalbeascoa describes, Spain has a strong lineage of exceptional modern architects, several of whom would have risen to international eminence if the country had not been so shunned during Franco's regime. Now, some of the inheritors of that lineage are achieving that recognition though there are still others of comparable talent who have yet to do so. Rafael Moneo, for instance, is one of the handful of architects held in great esteem everywhere, while Enric Miralles, almost a generation younger, is one of the fastest rising stars in the international firmament. Yet José Antonio Martínez Lapeña and Elías Torres, who are between these two in age and have produced a string of magnificent works, enjoy only in Spain the renown they deserve.

Spanish architecture came to prominence pursuing a confident modernism that was most seductive because no longer possible elsewhere. Along with its utopian

8

social ideals, modernism had withered before a barrage of criticism for its insensitivities to history and context and for its social and technical failures, leaving only the lifeless husk of formulaic self-caricature in neo- and late modernism and high-tech. But modernism remained precisely apt to Spain's upbeat mood and aspirations. Besides, a major inspiration for modernism had been the white cubic compositions and outdoor lifestyle of traditional Spanish settlements. So now Spanish architects turned to modernism, particularly to such Scandinavians as Asplund and Aalto, who had drawn on both the high and vernacular architecture of Latin countries, to rediscover some Mediterranean essentials.

What excites about the best current Spanish architecture is that for all its minimalism and abstraction it still resonates with local context and history as well as larger Mediterranean themes. Hence it can even be convincingly urban. More than that, its avant-garde forms have the physical presence that comes from material solidity and tectonic integrity, all highlighted by a delicacy of detail possible only with handcrafting. All in all then Spanish architecture is still capable of creating an arresting sense of place, while the preference for hard, precise, and unadorned materials such as stone, steel, and concrete prevents any lapse into the merely picturesque.

If there is a consistent weakness in Spanish architecture, it is that its pursuit of the poetics of form and place is often at the expense of a precise attention to the particularities of programme. Nor, with some exceptions, is it particularly inventive in this respect. In the first flush of freedom it is the symbols of a new Spain that are being built—note that most of the buildings in this book are public. Except perhaps Enric Miralles, no architects are attempting the equivalents of the "social condensors" intended to provoke social and behavioral change, that were proposed in another newly liberated society by the Constructivists, whose forms influence so many young architects in Spain and elsewhere. But, then, as already noted, the particular strength of even the most astringently avant garde of Spanish architecture is that is is not so much disruptive as respectful of context and tradition. How long, though, the peculiar conditions on which this architecture thrives will last is open to question.

Buildings will inevitably become more industrial and less crafted. And already a more affluent and confident public is demanding that their tastes be met, and these are more conservative than those of the avant garde.

The positive qualities described above are of course most evident in the more mature architects. Rafael Moneo builds in many different contexts, but is always able to distill elements from local history and architecture to create buildings that though very palpably rooted in place and present also cement connections back and forth in time and space. The other older architect in this idiosyncratic selection, Manuel Gallego, has in contrast worked almost entirely in his native Galicia and his architecture is more obviously modern and regionalist than Moneo's.

The next pair of practices in terms of chronological age have strong links with Moneo. Josep Llinás, with Martínez Lapeña and Torres, all consider teaching as assistants to Moneo as crucial to finding their own distinctive approaches. Martínez Lapeña/Torres's architecture veers between the inventively playful and the rationally sober, though both extremes are equally refined and often found in the same work. Some of Llinás's work has affinities with the sober architecture of this pair. But the work of both practices is very much generated from the specifics of place. Both also are fans of Gaudí's sometime collaborator, Josep Maria Jujol, whose quirky spirit continues also in the work of Miralles and Alfredo Arribas. Barcelonans all, they share a distinct Catalan spirit displayed in both their rather surreal humor and their inventiveness with form and construction, and, found also in Santiago Calatrava (who has various affinities with Gaudí) and Enric Battle and Joan Roig.

Other than the Madrileño Alberto Campo Baeza, whose work tends to a graphic abstractness, the architects in this selection have not yet forged for themselves approaches so distinctly either Spanish or personal, with all outside influences thoroughly digested. Their selection is more of an act of faith on the part of Zabalbeascoa. This gives a real freshness to the choice, especially as several are still unknown outside of Spain. And who knows, the choice may prove astutely prescient.

Architects' Biographies

Alfredo Arribas (b. Barcelona, 1954) studied at ETSAB (the architecture school of Barcelona), where he received his degree in 1977. He has been teaching in this school for over twelve years, and is also a member of the board of directors at Elisava, Barcelona's reputed design school. He was president of the Catalan interior design association, INFAD, from 1982 to 1985. In 1987, Arribas joined with the architect Miguel Morte and established their studio as Alfredo Arribas, Arquitectos Asociados. Arribas has been awarded several prizes for both his architecture and his interior design. Among them: the 214 housing units commissioned by MOPU (1981), with Basilio Tobías; the 1987 FAD prize for his Network Café, with Eduard Samsó; and the 1988 FAD prize for his Louie Vega Discotheque. Alfredo Arribas was a finalist for the FAD prize in 1990, with his Jane Greystoke chair. In this same year, he was awarded the FAD Gold Medal in recognition of his excellent professional career. Recent projects, such as the Spanish Pavilion at the Buchmesse '91 in Frankfurt, and an amusement park in Rimini, Italy, have brought his firm international recognition.

Iñaki Avalos (b. San Sebastián, 1956) and **Juan Herreros** (b. San Lorenzo del Escorial, 1958) received their architecture degrees from ETSAM, the architecture school of Madrid, where both now teach. They became partners in 1984. Avalos and Herreros are co-authors of *Le Corbusier Skyscrapers*, which received a prize from COAM, the Madrid architectural association, in 1988. They are currently working on a book on the technical and conceptual evolution of commercial architecture in Spain. In 1987, they won the competition to build a housing unit at the M-30 Motorway in Madrid and, in 1989, they were chosen to design a new office building for Renfe (the Spanish railway company) in Madrid.

Enric Batlle (b. Barcelona, 1956) and **Joan Roig** (b. Barcelona, 1954) graduated from ETSAB (the architecture school of Barcelona) in 1979. They now both teach there. Before becoming partners in 1981, the two had worked in the studio of Elías Torres/José Antonio Martínez Lapeña. They have been awarded the first prize in the following competitions: Roques Blanques Cemetery, Barcelona, 1981; Municipal Park and Market in Alella, Barcelona, 1982; Pegaso Park, Barcelona, 1982; Plaza de España building, Alcañiz, Teruel, 1983; Sant Cugat Monastery Park, Barcelona, 1984; rehabilitation of the Santo Domingo Church, Alarcón, Madrid, 1984; rehabilitation of the Fontes Palace, Murcia 1985; Es Freginal Park in Mahón, Minorca, 1986; Bridge over Besós River, Barcelona, 1986; Park of the Rubí Castle, Barcelona, 1987. They have also been finalists in various international competitions, including the urbanization of Amiens and the design of a new bridge in Berlin.

Santiago Calatrava (b. Valencia, 1951) studied art and architecture in Valencia. From 1975 to 1979, he attended the Federal Polytechnic in Zurich, where he earned his engineering degree. In 1981, he received his doctorate in technical sciences and, in the same year, he opened his own architectural and engineering office in Zurich. He has participated in and won several international competitions, and has been the subject of monographic exhibitions in both Switzerland and Spain. In 1987, he was awarded the Auguste Perret UIA prize for applied technology in architecture. He has works in Switzerland, France, Spain, Great Britain, Germany, Canada, and the USA. Among his most recently won international competitions are the metro station in Valencia, the airport in Bilbao, the Bioshelter at the Cathedral of St. John the Divine in New York, the music hall in Tenerife, and the bridge over the Spree in Berlin.

Alberto Campo Baeza (b. Valladolid, 1946) graduated from ETSAM in 1971, and became associate professor of design at the school in 1976. He became the Madrid correspondent for the architectural magazine *A+U* in 1977, and obtained his doctoral degree in architecture in 1982. Campo has lectured in many universities around the world, including Cornell University, the University of Pennsylvania, La Faccoltá di Architettura di Milano, and ETH in Zurich, where he taught during the 1989–90 academic year. His work has been widely published and has received several prizes. The Turégano house was awarded a special prize in the World Biennale of Architecture held in Sophia, Bulgaria in 1989.

Jose Manuel Gallego Jorreto (b. Carballino, Orense, 1936) received his Architecture degree from ETSAM, the architecture school of Madrid, in 1963. In 1968, he received his doctoral degree from the same school. During his stay in Madrid, he worked in the studio of the rationalist architect Alejandro de la Sota, who has remained an important reference in Gallego's work. Gallego received two scholarships that allowed him to travel and study in Scandinavia and Paris in 1970. In 1974, he published the essay "Rural Architecture and Landscape" and, in 1977, a compilation of essays on "Landscape Formalization." Since 1979, he has taught at the school of architecture in La Coruña. Rural architecture and housing are fundamental to his work.

Josep Llinás (b. Barcelona, 1946) graduated from the school of architecture of Barcelona in 1969. He has been teaching design studios at the same school since 1970, as well as in ETSAV (the school of architecture of Vallés), since 1983. He has also lectured in several foreign architecture schools, such as the Architectural Association in London and the U.P.8. in Paris. During his student years, he worked in the studio of Josep María Coderch. His theoretical essays have been published in several magazines and books and he has also written a book on the modernist Catalan architect Josep María Jujol.

José Antonio Martínez Lapeña (b. Tarragona, 1941) and **Elías Torres** (b. Ibiza, 1944) both graduated from ETSAB, Barcelona's school of architecture, where they have been teaching for several years. Martínez Lapeña has also taught at ETSAV, the Vallés school of architecture, and Torres has been an instructor and lecturer at foreign universities such as the University of California in Los Angeles, and Harvard University's Graduate School of Design. In 1968, Torres and Martínez Lapeña opened their architectural firm. During more than twenty years of partnership, they have been awarded several prizes, among them four FAD prizes, and they have produced many exemplary buildings, such as the Boenders house in Ibiza, the remodeling of the old church of L'Hospitalet, also in Ibiza, the Mora d'Ebre Hospital, the house in Cap Martinet, Ibiza, and the future conference center to be built in Barcelona's Olympic Village.

Enric Miralles (b. Barcelona, 1955) and **Carme Pinós** (b. Barcelona, 1954) graduated from ETSAB, the architecture school of Barcelona, in 1978 and 1979, respectively. Miralles worked at Helio Piñón and Alberto Viaplana's studio from 1973 to 1984. He has been a visiting professor at several universities in the United States, the United Kingdom, Italy, and Austria. Currently, he is the chairman of the design department at Frankfurt's Städelschule. Pinós was awarded first prize in the Rural Housing competition of the Ministry of Public Works and Urbanism in 1982. In 1984, Miralles and Pinós became partners. Since then, they have won several prizes and competitions such as the headquarters for Artespaña, Barcelona; new city government building in Algemesí, Valencia; new cemetery, Igualada; sports center in Pollensa, Majorca; Parque de las Estaciones, Palma de Majorca; FAD prize for the interior design of La Llauna School, Badalona; sports palace in Huesca; and the new headquarters for the Círculo de Lectores in Madrid. Since 1985, Miralles and Pinós have given lectures on their work at the Architectural Association in London, OAF in Oslo, BAF in Bergen, Columbia University in New York, Washington University in St. Louis, TAF in Norway, A.A. in Siena, TV in Berlin, Harvard University in Cambridge, Massachusetts, and the University of Southern California in Los Angeles, among others. Their work has been exhibited in several monographic shows in New York, Stuttgart, and Paris.

Rafael Moneo (b. Tudela, Navarra, 1937) graduated from ETSAM (the Madrid school of architecture) in 1961. While a student, he worked for Saenz de Oíza and later for Jorn Urtzon in Denmark. In 1963, Moneo received a scholarship that allowed him to spend two years studying at the Spanish Academy in Rome. His visit to the Italian city was to remain a fundamental influence in his work and professional career. Back in Spain, he taught at the school of architecture in Barcelona (ETSAB) before initiating a period of teaching and lecturing in several universities: Princeton, Lausanne, Cambridge, Architecture Association of London, ETH Zurich, Cooper Union School of Architecture in New York, and Harvard University's Graduate School of Design, where he was chairman of the department of architecture from 1985 to 1990. Moneo is a contributor to several architecture periodicals and a collection of his essays is to be published in two volumes. Among his most interesting built projects are the Bankinter building in Madrid, with Ramón Bescós (1973), the Logroño town hall (1981), the Roman Museum in Mérida, Spain, (1980–84), the Prevision Española in Seville (1982–87), and the Banco de Jaén (1983–88). Moneo recently won international competitions for an art and architecture museum in Stockholm, and the new Palazzo del Cinema in Venice.

César Portela (b. Pontevedra,1937) graduated from ETSAB, the architecture school of Barcelona, in 1966. Two years later, he received his doctorate from the same school. He has been teaching in the architecture school of La Coruña since 1983. In 1982 he was nominated as the Spanish candidate for the Pritzker Prize. The same year he received a gold medal from the European Council for his rehabilitation of the Concello house. In 1990 he was awarded the Critique Prize in Representation Arts. He has won several architecture competitions to restore and rehabilitate public areas and urban or rural spaces in his native region of Galicia. More recently, he was invited to participate in a closed competition to design the Spanish Pavilion at the 1992 World Expo in Seville.

José Luis Solans (b. Zaragoza, 1951), **Pilar Briales** (b. Madrid, 1953), and **Ricardo del Amo** (b. Mahón, 1954) graduated from ETSAM, the architecture school of Madrid, in 1977, 1984, and 1982, respectively. Solans also spent two years in economic and law schools. Since 1977, he has been an instructor of building acoustics in Madrid's school. Solans and Briales opened their studio in 1977, and three years later, del Amo joined them after having worked in several other studios. Together, they have won four competitions: the city planning of various small villages in Zaragoza and Teruel (1983); the rehabilitation of the Meteorological Institute in Madrid (1984); the re-design of the San Cristóbal square in Salamanca (1985); and the Madrid Pavilion for the 1992 World Expo of in Seville. Interested in designing comprehensive architecture, Solans, Briales, and del Amo have produced several furniture and interior designs. They have lectured extensively in many Spanish universities, and have organized seminars and courses on art and architecture.

Pep Zazurca (b. Barcelona, 1955) received his architectural degree in 1979. In 1988, he won the competition for the Carles I Park, at the Olympic Village in Barcelona. He also won first prize in the competition to remodel the field hockey stadium in Tarrasa, in preparation for the Olympic Games. In 1989, he was awarded the Puig i Cadafalch architecture prize.

THE JOURNEY TO MODERNITY

Anatxu Zabalbeascoa

"All built or projected architecture is significant of its context."
Antonio Fernández Alba, *La Crisis de la Arquitectura Española*, 1972

The Beginning of Modernity

"The primordial instinct of every human being is to secure himself a shelter."
Le Corbusier, *Vers une Architecture*, 1923

THE GATEPAC (Grupo de Arquitectos y Técnicos Españoles para la Arquitectura Contemporánea) was created in Zaragoza in 1930. This association of architects was fundamental in promoting in Spain the ideas of the Modern Movement, which later evolved into the so-called International Style. This imported trend found a large number of followers in Spain, especially in Barcelona and Madrid, who constituted what was later to be called the rationalist movement in Spain. This first group of modern architects was led by Josep Lluis Sert, who later became dean of Harvard University's Graduate School of Design, and José Torres Clavé and Rodriguez Arias in Barcelona. García Mercadal led the Madrid group, while José Mª de Aizpurúa, from San Sebastián, played a similar role in the northern regions. Aizpurúa died, however, soon after the Spanish Civil War started. With the war, not only men died, but also the ideals and even the ideas.

From 1936 until the end of the war in 1939, there was, logically, a period of little architectural activity in Spain, since these were years of destruction rather than construction. When the Fascist group that had won the war imposed Franco as dictator of the country, the rationalist, utopian, Bauhausian ways being investigated before the conflict were of little interest to the recently risen *Caudillo*, who hoped to return to the imperial architecture that had characterized the rich and splendorous years of the ancient empires.

After the Civil War, with Franco in power, GATEPAC dissolved—understanding the implications of the prevailing antidemocratic and rather imperialistic ideals of the new regime for architecture. Indeed, there was very little this association had to do with an empire, and, as Fernández Alba stated, the rationalist architects who did not die on the battlefields abandoned their rationalist ideology in order to concentrate on their own survival.

During Franco's first years in power, there was a strong revisionist architectural movement. It was the beginning of an era of nostalgia for a splendor that was lost, sometimes before it had ever been known. The architecture sought by General Franco's regime was closer in spirit to ancient Roman civic constructions than it was to the German Nazi architecture of Albert Speer. History was revisited—allowing for the incorporation of quotations from styles associated with past empires of the "best" years in Western civilization. Architecture aimed to epitomize the government's expectations for the "new country" Spain was to become. Construction was the ideal political propaganda, although it would take several years to become visible. Unfortunately, the construction of large civic buildings was not enough to provide homes for all those in need. Long before anyone had talked about postmodernism and pastiche, the postwar right-wing government forced the implantation of such a style. In Spain, a known surrealist country, it could have been possible to talk about postmodernism before modernism. While most European countries were building sober, simple, and strictly functional architecture, under the rationalist avant-garde wave, in Spain public commissions were reconstructing the country in a neoclassical or neoimperial, pâpier-maché way.

In the late 1940s, once the country had begun to recover from the tremendous human and material losses of the war, new industrial demands had to be faced. In Europe, rationalism had succeeded under democratic regimes; therefore, although there was an urgent need for an architectural avant-garde in Spain, attempts to introduce Modern Movement architecture to schools and studios could not have succeeded. The original, democratic intentions of the movement were mistaken and confused, and rationalism in Spain became the consequence of the need for a new, more modern-looking architectural aesthetic rather than a reevaluation of the potential of the architect's role as a social mediator in such a vulnerable society.

In defense of the architects, it should be noted that levels of information and access to architectural documentation were minimal at this time, and, therefore, most professionals enjoyed only a very limited exposure to contemporary culture. The lack of national publications, the very active censorship established by General Franco's dictatorship, and the fact that hardly anyone was able to read foreign-language publications were essential factors contributing to this situation. Additionally, and most dramatically, most of the books and journals in the Madrid Architecture Library had been used to build barricades when the battle lines had moved to the University area and, consequently, had been destroyed.

1. Francisco Cabrero, Union Delegation Building, Madrid, 1949

General Franco's government did everything it could to prevent the end of the imperial construction era, seeing this as a premonition of the end of its own "empire." Several examples of Spanish architecture produced during this period reflect this lack of communication, the isolationism, and the classicist tendency imposed by the government. Within this atmosphere, the language of the Modern Movement was adopted for the design of some bourgeois houses, as an aesthetic style rather than out of social necessity. The Bauhausian aspects incorporated in some works were, therefore, purely emblematic since this type of simple functionalist construction as produced in Spain was not the product of social demand. As a result, the small number of projects following the modern movement paradigm built in Spain during this period cannot claim to have addressed important social issues such as integration, housing, or even general improvement.

Among the notable projects produced at this time, several architects and buildings deserve special recognition, not only because they represent the rationalist era in the history of Spanish architecture, but also because of their proven influence on later, younger generations.

Francisco de Asis Cabrero's Union Delegation Building (1) in Madrid (1949) marks a stylistic bridge between the aforementioned intentionally imperialistic, official architecture and the new modern era. Although

13

2. Francisco Cabrero, Feria del Campo pavilion, Madrid, 1965

3. Josep Mª Sostres, Agustí house, 1955

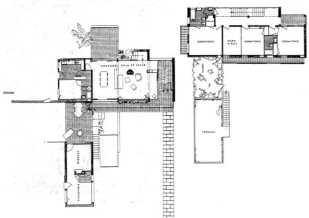

4. Josep Mª Sostres, plans for Agustí house, 1955

5. Josep Mª Coderch, Barceloneta Apartments, Barcelona, 1951

Cabrero's work has the severe quality of the best rationalism *(2)* (Palacio de Cristal, the Arriba Newspaper building), his work, like that produced by most of the practicing architects of the time, reveals the conservative ideals of the only leading political party. Like most rationalist architects of the period, such as Miguel Fisac, who received many private sector commissions, Josep Mª Sostres *(3, 4)*, who maintained a very critical position toward what was being built in the country, and Javier Carvajal, J. Cano Lasso, and Josep María Coderch, Cabrero came from a bourgeois family that shared, to a great extent, the regime's conservative ideals. It is of interest to note that, like other modern architects working under non-democratic regimes (e.g., Giuseppe Terragni), Josep Mª Coderch spent the last ten years of his life researching a new urban housing system, in which each dwelling would be autonomous in spite of the collective functioning of the whole building.

Of this generation, Coderch, who once modestly pointed out that he owed his prestige to the very low architectural level of others, has been a major influence on later generations. His Barceloneta Apartments *(5, 6)* proposed a spatial layout much admired and reinterpreted by younger architects (Martínez Lapeña/Torres, Campo Baeza, etc.). Fisac and his use of reinforced concrete was an important influence in the work of Javier Carvajal, Daniel Gelabert, and later, Miralles/Pinós and Zazurca (compare, for instance, the lighting system used in the latter's remodeling of the Concepción School in Barcelona and that used in Fisac´s Asunción School *[8]*). Alejandro de la Sota, who made the International Style

14

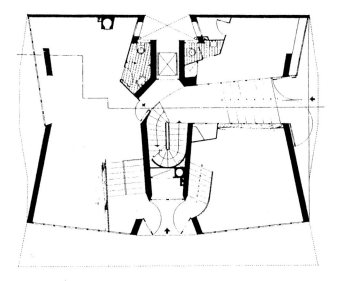

7. *Alejandro de la Sota, Government Building, Tarragona, 1957*

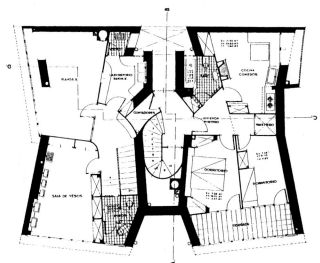

8. *Miguel Fisac, Asunción School, Madrid, 1965*

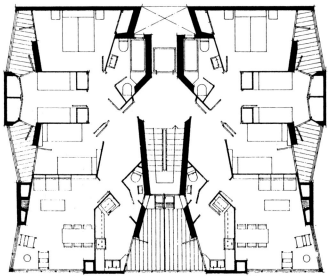

6. *Coderch, plans for Barceloneta Apartments, Barcelona, 1951*

"official" by winning the competition for a government building in Tarragona in 1957 (7), may also be seen as a major influence on younger architects such as Llinás and Gallego, inheritors of his perfect volumes, strong textures, and plasticity of voids.

The Spanish Pavilion by José Antonio Corrales and Ramón Vázquez Molezún, built in Brussels for the 1958 World's Fair *(9)* remains another fundamental example of the Modern Movement in Spanish architecture.

15

9. *José Antonio Corrales and Ramón Vázquez Molezún, Spanish pavilion for the World Expo, Brussels, 1958*

10. *Martorell, Bohigas and Mackay, Meridiana building, Barcelona, 1965*

Organicism and Realism

"What fine, really dignified attempt do we have here in Spain? Anything that can truly be interesting as architecturally ours and of real value? It is sad, but I believe there is very little, so we have covered Spain with dull pitiful architecture. Scarce imagination and little seriousness. It is sad to be where any healthy attempt is suffocated."
Alejandro de la Sota, in *Revista Nacional de Arquitectura*, 1954

The second rationalist generation in Spain applied the carefully learned notions of very simple, geometric volumes and non-ornamental, functional architecture to the popular and traditional ways of building in the different Spanish regions.

Early in the 1950s, the so-called Grupo R sought a renaissance of the indigenous Catalan architectural culture. Aiming to mix tradition with modernity, it began to search for a new Catalan school of architecture able to combine tradition with the contemporaneous language supported by the Modern Movement doctrine. In the 1960s, a younger generation of architects including Josep Martorell, Federico Correa, Alfonso Milá, Studio Per,

Domenech and Amadó, Ricardo Bofill, Sabater, Rodrigo and Cantallops, and loosely led by Oriol Bohigas, organized a new group that wanted to combine rationalist ideals with a certain local reality: the Catalan tradition. This group was to be called the Escuela de Barcelona (Barcelona school) and intended to break away from the architectural establishment toward a more realistic and communicative architecture. Their commissions came from the private sector. Public commissions at this time were still under the control of Franco's regime and were generally given to Madrid architects, since most of these works were built in the Madrid area. Martorell, Bohigas and Mackay's Meridiana building *(10)* became an important example for many younger architects—somewhat like a catalogue of possible architectural solutions. In fact, the work this firm produced during this period remains its most interesting contribution to Spanish modern architecture.

Domenech and Amadó's apartment building on the Costa Brava *(11)* represents the Barcelona school's ideals of rationalism and realism applied to the Catalan landscape. Ricardo Bofill, one of the most promising members of the school, was awarded the prestigious FAD (Fomento de las Artes Decorativas—Fostering the

16

11. Domenech/Amadó, apartment building, Costa Brava, 1970

12. Ricardo Bofill, apartment, Nicaragua Street, Barcelona, 1965

13. Saenz de Oíza, Torres Blancas building, Madrid, 1968

nized and more personal level. Fullaondo tried to group certain Madrid architects around the *Nueva Forma* (New form) magazine, so that a new Madrid architectural school could be organized. A more organic approach, which followed Bruno Zevi's theories and urgings to break away from and improve Modern Movement designs, was the key to the new architectural attitude in Madrid. With Corbusier and Wright as clear references, Saenz de Oíza's Torres Blancas building in Madrid *(13)* is perhaps the best example of this period. Learning and inheriting both methods and materials from the old Castilian building tradition, Iñiguez de Ozoño, F. Higueras, A. Miró, and Fernández Alba produced an organized architecture that melded the two complementary principles of novelty and tradition.

The Seventies: Bridge to Democracy

"Clean up city center and monumentalize the periphery."
Oriol Bohigas, 1981

By the early 1970s, some architectural theorists had already begun to predict a future of eclectic architectural production.

Decorative Arts) architecture prize for his apartment building in Barcelona's Nicaragua Street *(12)*. In subsequent projects, Bofill chose other paths, and his scandalous and even aggressive work, inspired by a nostalgia for the imperial years, similar to the revisionist architecture produced under Franco, seems to be just a parody of those projects.

In Madrid, attempts to connect with the international architectural avant-garde took place at a less orga-

17

Antimodernism summarizes the position adopted by the many Spanish architects in the early 1970s who left behind the organicism of the Madrid School and the realism of the Barcelona School. New values were aroused, and architects began to separate from the centralized groups and move toward their own individualized styles. Saenz de Oíza, the author of one of the best examples of late Spanish organicism, designed an elegant glazed tower that had very little to do with the baroque style of Torres Blancas. The new Banco de Bilbao tower *(14)*, together with Cabrero's offices for the Arriba newspaper *(15)*, de la Sota's Maravillas gymnasium, and Corrales and Molezún's Bankunión building *(16)*, all in Madrid, are the last examples of Spanish modernist architecture.

The Bankinter building *(17)* in Madrid (1973) by Rafael Moneo and Ramón Bescós, serves as a link between modernism and a new eclectic, individualistic era, with modernist principles as the point of departure . Formal continuity, the use of a contextual ornamental vocabulary, and the incorporation of a compositional order similar to that of the surrounding buildings were keys to this new architecture that aimed to build cities by integration rather than by opposing existing constructions. In this

15. Francisco Cabrero, Arriba building, Madrid, 1965

14. Francisco Saenz de Oíza, Banco de Bilbao, Madrid, 1979

16. Corrales/Molezún, Bankunión building, Madrid, 1975

18

17. Rafael Moneo/Ramón Bescós, Bankinter building, Madrid, 1973

18. José Ignacio Linazasoro and Miguel Garay, housing, Mendigorría, 1980

respect, Linazasoro and Garay's houses at Mendigorría *(18)* worked from a rationalist schema to create a new adaptation and recognition of their surroundings.

The International Style had become obsolete. Possible new approaches to architecture—whether eclectic and respectful of context and tradition, or more conceptual and abstract with strong neoplasticist and constructivist links—would lead eventually, and after several years of experimentation, to postmodernism on one hand and to deconstructivism on the other. This period, characterized by what Ignasi de Solá Morales has called "the loss of avant-garde illusion," produced individuals in search of innovative forms in architecture.

In Madrid, projects such as the Adriática building by Javier Carvajal *(19)*, the aforementioned Bankinter building, and Saenz de Oíza's Banco de Bilbao tower characterized the beginning of an era during which architects such as the De las Casas brothers *(20)*, Jerónimo Junquera and Estanislao Pérez Pita, known for their public housing buildings, Javier Carvajal and Julio Cano Lasso, together with some early works of Campo Baeza, Victor López Cotelo, and Carlos Puente, were to play a major role.

In Barcelona, Martorell, Bohigas and Mackay abandoned their own realist and localist architecture to embrace a new period of plasticity of form and more strictly geometrical volumes. Their Thau School *(21)* exemplifies this new attitude. Works by Viaplana and Piñón, Esteve Bonell, Studio Per (Clotet, Cirici, Bonet, and Tusquets), Jaume Bach and Gabriel Mora, Jordi Garcés, and Enric Soria are paradigmatic of this new era that wanted to join modernism with a rather uncertain eclecticism. The house at Pantelleria *(22)* by Tusquets and Clotet is one of the best examples of an architecture that, by applying local, past references, was able to create a masterpiece.

In Seville, the competition to build the new Andalusian Architectural Association headquarters was a milestone in this town's architectural history. Many of the best known architects of the time entered the competition, which was won by Gabriel Ruiz Cabrero and Enrique Perea *(23)*, with a brilliant building that played a role similar to that of Moneo's Bankinter building in Madrid: it was the natural bridge between Modern

19. Javier Carvajal, Adriática building, Madrid, 1981

21. Martorell, Bohigas, Mackay, Thau School, Barcelona, 1974

20. De las Casas, Palomares Public Housing, Madrid, 1979

22. Oscar Tusquets and Lluis Clotet, house, Pantelleria, 1975

23. Cabrero and Perea, Architectural Association, Seville, 1982

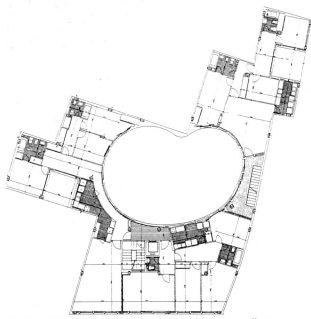

24. Cruz/Ortiz, housing on María Coronel Street, Seville, 1973

25. Cruz/Ortiz, housing on María Coronel Street, Seville, 1973

26. Miguel Prada Pool, "Instant City," Ibiza, 1970

27. Miguel Prada Pool, "Instant City," Ibiza, 1970

Movement ideals and the increasing concern for creating cities by contributing to their urbanism. Also in Seville, architects such as Guillermo Vázquez Consuegra, Ramón Sierra, and the Cruz/Ortiz studio were very active in reconstructing the city. Public housing was of special importance. The housing project at María Coronel Street by Cruz/Ortiz (24, 25) was an excellent *opera prima*, a herald of what these architects would produce in the future.

Also of note during this period is the work of a small

number of architects, among whom Miguel Prada Poole is of special importance. This group had been producing, for quite a long time, "futuristic" architecture, which used folded prefabricated structures, man-made materials, and other new technologies. These architects, who believed the recent incorporation of computers as design tools could safeguard against a predictable revisionist panorama, were generally misunderstood by their contemporaries, and their work remained largely theoretical. Prada Poole's prefabricated modular structures *(26, 27)*, used as temporary buildings for the Pamplona Art Meetings in 1970, are excellent examples of a very realistic and well elaborated architecture that could have had an impact in a growing country like Spain. Due to other commercial interests, this type of industrially produced construction was used and remained as temporary architecture.

The Eclectic Eighties

"Art forms created by transgression are filled by nostalgia. When architects wanted to transgress the language of the International Style, they could only resort to recourse in a panoply of historicisms."
Peter Halley, *After Art*

Since General Franco's death in November 1975, the Spanish public administration has played a major role in the encouragement and support of a new generation of architects with a new avant-garde spirit, as well as in the revitalization of cities. Most of the newly elected central, regional, and municipal representatives were former left-wing leaders who had been critical of the previous undemocratic regime. Within this atmosphere, it was considerably easier to promote an architecture of change. A radical change was what was needed, and, indeed, "change" seems to have been on of the most widely used words in Spain after November 20, 1975.

Postmodernism, the international art and architecture movement of the 1980s, did not find many followers in Spain. This was probably because, as stated above, there was such a pronounced need for change, and change was not likely to be best found by looking to the past for inspiration, as postmodernism did. In Spain, this movement fundamentally influenced the work of only four major architecture firms. Ricardo Bofill, once the *enfant terrible* architect from Barcelona, with several studios around the world, produced an architecture aiming to return tradition to the people, and intending to repair the "poor," functional simplicity and lack of ornament the International Style had imposed on the architectural vocabulary. Bofill's style, like that of Charles Moore, Michael Graves, and many other postmodern architects,

28. Ricardo Bofill, INEF Building, Barcelona, 1991

29. *Oscar Tusquets, housing, Más Abelló, 1990*

was revivalist. He recreated imperial buildings, transforming them into public housing without really changing the basic arrangement of the old working-class family dwelling. Public housing was not an ideal field for postmodernists, for it was not long before people felt cheated by seeing familiar housing spaces covered with an imperial appearance. Bofill's frequent recreations of a classical Greek temple (Teatro Nacional de Cataluña, INEF building *[28]*) have enabled him to develop an innovative architecture and to realize the improvement this type of building has undergone since the time it refers to.

Similar options have been chosen by Oscar Tusquets in his latest works *(29)*. His house in the Maresme, where historic references are used in an attempt to recapture the beauty and calm of past styles, is a good example of this architect's connection to the international postmodern attitude. On the other hand, Tusquets has proven to be a tireless and very fine industrial designer, with increasing work for internationally known companies such as Alessi *(30)*, Driade, and Cleto Munari in Italy, and Casas and B.D. in Spain. His former partner, Lluis Clotet, has also experimented with postmodern trends in his recent work, such as the Banco de España in Gerona.

30. *Oscar Tusquets, Alessi teapot*

31. Francisco Saenz de Oíza, auditorium, Santander, 1991

Finally, the work of Francisco Saenz de Oíza, a recognized organicist and modern master, can probably fit under this postmodern heading as well. His Santander Auditorium *(31)* reveals clear references to James Stirling's design for the Stuttgart National Gallery, proving once again Saenz de Oíza's ability to connect with prevailing international trends. While some of his other work, such as the organicist Torres Blancas and the late-modern Banco de Bilbao, both in Madrid, clearly refer to earlier stylistic movements, his recent housing project at the Madrid M-30 Motorway incorporates some of the above-mentioned postmodernist features.

Some of the latest work of Martorell, Bohigas and Mackay can also, strangely enough, be included in this section. Their house in Son Vida, Majorca *(32)*, incorporates possibly the most varied techniques, materials, and formal relations found in an eclectic architecture.

Aside from the group of Spanish architects who chose the postmodernist dogmas, ideas, and implications to build new credos, there is another group of architects, headed by Rafael Moneo, who have expressed in a different manner their concern and respect for the surrounding context and the history, culture, plasticity, geometry,

ornament, and traditions of these contexts. Moneo's work shows clear references to and respect for its geographical location. In spite of this, his architecture does not belong to a particular context, like that of his colleagues of the Basque and Galician regions. Moneo's architecture helps build the city. His most recent buildings, the Kursaal Auditorium in San Sebastián, the Previsión Insurance Building in Seville *(33)*, and the Seville Airport *(34)* have continued the contextualization started in the Roman Museum in Mérida *(35)*. Moneo's works evolve to adapt to very different situations, smoothly fitting their geographical location and culture. This architect's work carries that rare quality of being at once Moneo and Seville, Moneo and Barcelona, Moneo and San Sebastián, Moneo and Palma de Mallorca, Mérida, Massachusetts, Venice, or wherever his commissions are to stand. Rather than being an author's architecture or an architecture where buildings are treated as isolated objects, his is a committed architecture of an author, building, program, and place.

When discussing Spanish architects of international acclaim, it is a pity not to be able to include in that group Juan Navarro Baldeweeg *(36, 37)* and Martínez Lapeña

32. Martorell, Bohigas and Mackay, house in Son Vida, Majorca, 1988

and Torres *(38–41)*. Although they have received some small international attention, their work—as seen in the former's House of the Rain or the remodelling of the Segura Mills, and in the latter's houses in Ibiza or the Mora d'Ebre Hospital—undoubtedly deserves wider recognition, both for the pioneering of spatial layouts and the daring plasticity of the forms.

The work of the Cruz/Ortiz studio and Guillermo Vázquez Consuegra in Seville; Linazasoro and Peña Ganchegui and Javier Cenicacelaya in the Basque region; Manuel Gallego and César Portela in Galicia; and Vetges tu i Mediterránea in the Valencia area may also be grouped under the sector led by Moneo, since all share a similar interest in and respect for contextual culture, traditions, architectonic volumes, and styles.

In the 1980s there was a third position among architects whose work had more to do with architecture than with context. Supporting an idea of progress and originality, and using man-made materials, these architects understood the building as an isolated object, detached from its context. The source of the ideas of this new gen-

34. Rafael Moneo, airport, Seville, 1991

eration is a combination of Alejandro de la Sota's well-learned and applied rational experience with the more conceptual ways explored by Piñón and Viaplana. Their Plaza de Sants *(42, 43)* has proven to be a fundamental project in the evolution of recent Spanish architecture,

33. Rafael Moneo, Previsión Insurance Building, Seville, 1987

35. Rafael Moneo, Roman Museum, Mérida, 1984

where a more conceptual approach, the formal expression of an industrial era, is able to dignify by shocking contrast an otherwise devastated urban context. The Plaza dels Paisos Catalans, or Plaza de Sants, was the beginning of the *plazas duras* ("hard" squares) series of constructions which, supported by urbanistic policies initiated by Oriol Bohigas, as the new head of the Barcelona Department of Urban Design, aimed to transform the Catalan capital through multiple small interventions.

The Plaza de Sants was also the project that gained national recognition for Enric Miralles. Shortly after-

ward, he started his own studio, with Carme Pinós as partner, and has produced some of the most avant-garde architecture designed in Spain in recent years.

Some of Josep Llinás's work *(44–46)*, because of its clever, smoothly elegant adaptation to the urban context, can be included with the work of those led by Moneo. However, some of Llinás's projects refer back to de la Sota and can thus also be included in this last section of those who have chosen to embrace deconstructivism. Zazurca's deconstructions and use of industrial materials indicate *(47)* that he, too, is clearly aware of the interna-

36. *Juan Navarro Baldeweeg, Molinos del Segura, Murcia, 1990*

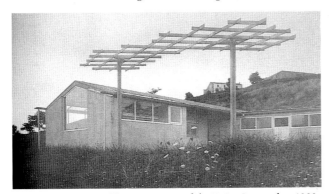

37. *Juan Navarro Baldeweeg, House of the Rain, Santander, 1982*

38. *Martínez Lapeña/Torres, hardware store, Ibiza, 1986*

tional panorama of the 1980s.

Santiago Calatrava's functional organicism *(48)* and Alfredo Arribas's work *(49)* might be grouped together. Although the former is best known as an engineer and the latter as an interior designer, their work shares similar essences, in which anatomical references and the use of state-of-the-art technology are fundamental design tools. Calatrava's interest in anatomy—particulary animal and human skeletons—may have an engineering explanation, since the body is a quasi-perfect construction. Arribas's interest in the same bony structures may refer to Antoni Gaudí's and Catalan modernism's employment of sensuous, organic references, which has influenced many Catalan architects.

The late 1980s in Spain have been characterized by the work of a new generation of architects. These years have been marked by the increasing number of competitions they have won and the ever-growing number of projects they are working on. This new generation of young architects, mostly in their thirties, (Carme Pinós and Enric Miralles *[50]*, Emilio Tuñón, Joan Roig and Enric

39. Martínez Lapeña/Torres, Hospital Mora d'Ebre, Tarragona, 1987

40. Martínez Lapeña/Torres, Hospital Mora D'Ebre, 1987

41. Martínez Lapeña/Torres, Hospitalet Church, Ibiza, 1984

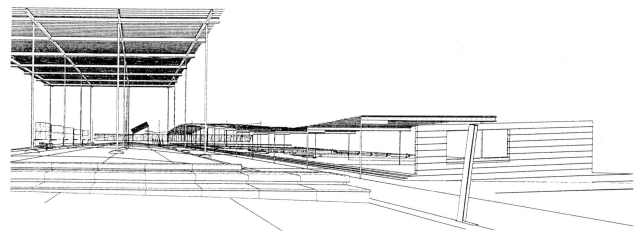

42. Piñón/Viaplana, Plaza de Sants, Barcelona, 1983

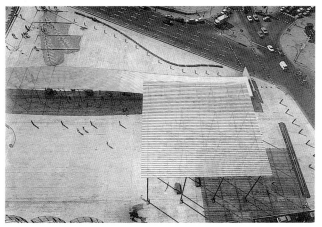

43.Piñón/Viaplana, Plaza de Sants, Barcelona, 1983

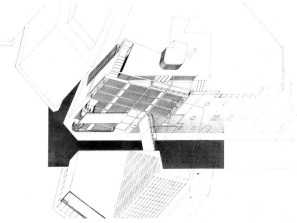

45. Josep Llinás, Architectural Association Competition

44. Josep Llinás, house in Bagur, Barcelona, 1980

46. Josep Llinás, plan for school, Barcelona, 1991

31

47. Pep Zazurca, Dos Torres Bar, Barcelona, 1988

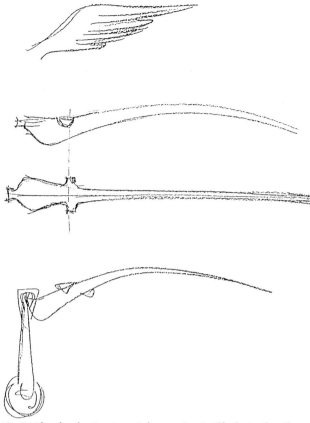

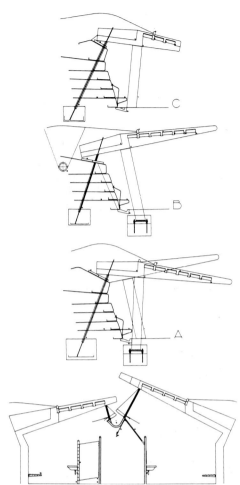

48, 49. *Sketches by Santiago Calatrava (top), Alfredo Arribas (bottom)*

50. *Enric Miralles/Carme Pinós, sketch*

51. *Iñaki Avalos/Juan Herreros, construction detail, Telefónica*

52. *Avalos/Herreros, Telefónica building proposal, 1989*

Batlle, José Antonio Val, Iñaki Avalos and Juan Herreros [51, 52], Pep Zazurca, Yago Conde, and Alfredo Arribas, among others) is mostly concentrated around the urban areas of Madrid and Barcelona, Spain's largest cities. If there is anything, besides their age, which could group these professionals in the same category, it is the possibility of including them in what can be called the "trans-modern" or "neo-modern" group. Having rejected historicist revisions, they all acknowledge their debt to the Modern Movement. Although they do not accept the dogmatism of its principles, which they have studied, under-

stood, and absorbed, they have learned how to transform them through their own doctrines, interpretations, and additions.

The very recent international trend, "deconstructivism" or neomodernism, loosely based on Jacques Derrida's philosophical arguments and exemplified in the work of Zaha Hadid, Coop Himmelblau, Peter Eisenman,

55. *Pep Zazurca, Z house, Barcelona, 1991*

and Daniel Libeskind, among others, has played an important role for the younger generation. The projects of the youngest Spanish architects replicate not necessarily these influences, but rather the abstraction of the idea supporting them. Rebuilding architecture means to them providing the basis for a new language by looking to the future, rather than to the past. The work of Miralles/Pinós *(53)*, Zazurca *(55)*, and Solans/Briales/del Amo *(54)* reveals the arrival of these ideas in Spain.

New Spanish Architecture

"...in order to take part in modern civilization, it is necessary at the same time to take part in scientific, technical, and political rationality, something which very often requires the pure and simple abandon of a whole cultural past. It is a fact: every culture cannot sustain and absorb the shock of modern civilization. There is the paradox: how to become modern and to return to sources; how to revive an old, dormant civilization and take part in universal civilization..." Paul Ricoeur, *Universal Civilization and National Cultures*, 1961

53. *Miralles/Piños, La Llauna School, Badalona, 1986*

56. *Manuel Gallego, Gallego house, La Coruña, 1979*

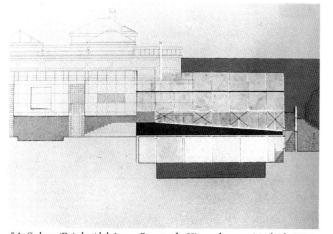

54. *Solans/Briales/del Amo, Puerta de Hierro house, Madrid, 1982*

57. *Portela, Caballería de Santaniña, La Coruña, 1988*

Current architectural production in Spain is not defined by temporal lines of demarcation but, rather, by each architect's individual characteristics. Therefore, and after careful study and a painstaking selection procedure, the author has tried to group concisely those who, in her personal opinion, best represent the most avant-garde of contemporary Spanish architecture.

Together with a younger generation of professionals under forty, the selection includes Elías Torres/José Antonio Martínez Lapeña and Rafael Moneo, under fifty and over fifty respectively, as the acknowledged masters of the previous generation. They are the teachers, leaders, and models of the younger generation because of and through the continuous renovation of their architecture.

Gallego *(56)* and Portela *(57)*, from the Galician region, have been chosen for what their architecture represents. Because of the importance of tradition and the attention paid to local context and social concerns, their architecture reflects a high level of maturity. Although their work cannot be defined as an international model, due to the strong links that relate their constructions to the existing geographical context, the abstraction of their work, and the concept of readjusting valid modern principles to specific locations, deserves international recognition.

Josep Llinás can be seen as the Catalan link between two extremely productive generations: the studios that originated around and later departed from the Barcelona school (Garcés and Soria, Bach and Mora, Carlos Ferrater) and the following generation (Xavier Vendrell; Batlle and Roig; Ribas and Ravetllat *[58]*; Viader; Soto; Tuñón; Arriola; Mangado Beloqui *[59]*, Arenas and Basiana; Navas and Solé *[61]*; Miralles and Pinós). Perhaps Victor Rahola also performs a connective role, similar to that of Llinás, in the Catalan architectural panorama.

Finally, Alberto Campo Baeza *(60)* has been

35

58. *Ribas/Ravetllat, entry to soccer field, Barcelona, 1990*

59. *Mangado Beloqui, Olite Square, Navarra, 1989*

60. *Alberto Campo Baeza, Town Hall, Fene, La Coruña, 1980*

included as a major representative and inheritor of the Modern Movement. Also from the previous generation, his talented, simple, and economical works have evolved coherently and rigorously with his ideals. Although he has not produced new concepts, spatial layouts, or technological applications, his appropriate and elegant use of materials, floor plan arrangements, and severe geometric volumes deserve close attention.

The group of architects under forty are the pupils of the preceding generation and they have all had access to international trends. Although they began their studies in architecture under Franco's regime, the end of the undemocratic era in Spain was arriving at the time, and publications such as *Nueva Forma* in Madrid and *Arquitecturas Bis* in Barcelona developed a rigorous, intellectually challenging stance, which kept the new generation well informed. By the time these young architects started their own practices, General Franco had long been dead, and democracy, with all its implications, was developing new roots in the country. This new architectural group soon started its own journals, such as the refurbished *Quaderns* and *Arquitectura*, the new *El Croquis*, and *A-30* (produced by the above-mentioned group of architects around thirty years old), *Obradoiro, Tecnología y Arquitectura*, and *On*, where their theoretical contributions were published. However, unlike their predecessors, they chose and established their role as practitioners rather than theoreticians. They could maintain this position due to a steady flow of commissions from central and local governments and town halls before beginning to secure their own commissions from the private sector. The fact that the whole country needed to be reconditioned, re-modernized, and re-adapted to more contemporary needs (there was a lack of new schools, airports, stations, urban infrastructure, etc.) was, undoubtedly, a key contribution to making possible the steady professional practice of this new generation.

61. Daniel Navas & Neus Solé, Civic Center, Esparraguera, 1991

62. Xosé Bar Boo, Vázquez house, Galicia, 1963

The Other Regions

"Sustaining any kind of authentic culture in the future will depend ultimately on our capacity to generate vital forms of regional culture while appropriating alien influences at the level of both culture and civilization."

Kenneth Frampton, *Modern Architecture: A Critical History*, 1980

Galicia

The two urban areas around which the new Spanish architecture seems to be evolving are, for obvious reasons, Madrid and Barcelona. However, as the inclusion of two Galician architects in the book points out, there are other schools, other geographical areas, and other projects which, although they do represent very valuable architectural examples, usually investigate architectonic procedures already explored and experienced in the two primary urban centers, re-adapting them to their own local and cultural characteristics.

They are masters of the adaptation to their particular geographical context, needs, and tradition, similar to what, in the 1970s, was called the realist school. This ability to truly adapt to a particular context, has, undoubtedly, characterized some of the best examples in the history of architecture, and has also been a crucial feature in contemporary Galician architecture, as exemplified in the works of Portela and Gallego.

Besides Alejandro de la Sota, who, although born in Galicia, has always been associated with the most radical examples of rationalism built in Spain, another example of modernity may be found in the work of Xosé Bar Boo. His Vázquez house of 1963 *(62)*, however, is more of a trans-modern than a modern proposal, since it demonstrated a clear comprehension of International Style principles while at once challenging them.

Compared to some other Spanish regions, the architecture of this area has a strong local and traditional character. In this area, the *minifundio* (small parcel of land) is the system of land ownership, as opposed to the *latifundio* (large parcel of land), typically found in the southern regions of the Iberian Peninsula. Therefore, in this humid, northern area, public housing is of special importance. Several architects have analyzed, studied, written about and made proposals on this subject. The Housing for the Gypsies project *(63)*, designed by Pascuala Campos and César Portela in the 1970s, is an example of a way of dealing with the same problem that Manuel Gallego approached several years later in a different manner.

More recently, with an increasing interest in devel-

64. Xosé María Casabella, Pontes School, Galicia, 1963

63. Pascuala Campos/César Portela, Housing for the Gypsies, 1975

65. Xosé María Casabella, Pontes School, Galicia, 1963

66. Iago Seara, Casa Dominguez, Orense, 1987

67. J. Blanco, warehouse, Carballino, Orense, 1988

39

68. J. Blanco, urban sculpture, Carballino, Orense, 1989

70. Peña Ganchegui, housing, Motrico, 1965

69. Manuel Gallego, housing, Monticello, 1990

oping new architectural forms and criteria both in a social and in a formal sense, together with the economic revitalization of the mid-1980s, this geographical area has produced a number of other architectural examples of interest, like the more plasticist, slightly postmodern approach of Xosé María Casabella (64, 65), or the late-modern work of Iago Seara (66), as seen in his house for the fashion designer Adolfo Dominguez. A more universal path has been followed by some of the very young architects who have been strongly influenced by international news and trends. J. Blanco, with his use of angular forms, deconstruction of plans, and industrial materials, is Galicia's closest adherent to the deconstructivist style (67, 68).

Aside from these local interpretations of the international architectural panorama which undoubtedly have a very strong energy and quite a promising future, at this point the architecture of Manuel Gallego and César Portela summarizes, perhaps, the best work to be found in this area.

Gallego's work can be included in this section due

to the concern he has shown for public housing *(69)*, and the fact that he works to incorporate the culture and traditions of the area into his architecture. However, his designs are clearly indebted to the Modern Movement, which may be due to the years he spent in Alejandro de la Sota's studio. His architecture is therefore more extrapolative than the work by most of the architects from this region included here.

Basque Country

Geographically close to the Galician region and, therefore, sharing to a great extent its climate and vegetation, this region is also isolated from the rest of the Spanish peninsula, for it is located between the Cantabric Mountains and the Cantabric Sea, the latter being part of the same Atlantic Ocean that reaches the Galician coast.

These northern regions share similar humid climates, associated more with Europe's northern countries than with Spain. Cultural differences between these areas and other Spanish regions undoubtedly owe something to this fact. Euskadi, the Basque country, is, unlike Galicia, one of the most industrialized areas in Spain, with metallurgic industries, blast furnaces, fishing, and sea commerce which are possibly the basis for the strong, noble, reserved character that defines the inhabitants of the region.

In this splendid location there is not, however, an avant-garde contingent in architecture. There is no professional group identifiable as a collective or unified school with a shared ideology. Although there is a strong tendency toward a very rational construction, expressed by traditional forms and influenced by the customary indigenous materials (as exemplified in work by Luis Peña Ganchegui *[70–72]*, and, later, Miguel Garay, José Ignacio Linazasoro *[73]*, and possibly even Javier Cenicacelaya *[74]*, from the younger generation), there has not been an architectural avant-garde in this region since Peña Ganchegui's early works.

Rationalism arrived in this northern area through the work of José Manuel Aizpurúa (San Sebastián's yacht club) and Joaquín Layen (Sacha Café). Some other architects, such as Aguinaga, Vallejo, Arzadún and Unanue, can also be classified under the same functionalist label.

In the 1960s, rationalism was mixed with neo-brutalism, as can be seen in Martín Marcide's Hospital de Cruces, which follows international rather than local ideals. This short-lived trend was followed by a return to rationalist ideals, as exemplified in the work of Elías Más Serra, and Ramón Losada (Clínica Etxevarri) or Javier Salazar, in his El Fango municipal building.

Peña Ganchegui was the first Basque architect to receive national, and, later, international recognition. Seen at the time (the 1960s) as an outsider, classifiable neither in the organicist tendency of Madrid, nor in the collective realist impulse that was searching for a more culturally influenced rationalism in Barcelona, Peña

71. Peña Ganchegui, Peine de los Vientos waterfront park, 1976

Ganchegui apprehended and applied to his own context the principles defended by the Spanish organicist version of the Modern Movement. Peña's architecture is fundamentally Basque. It is about the Basque culture, country, traditions, beliefs, and character. His design work probably reached its excellence through his collaboration with another well-known Basque artist: the sculptor Eduardo Chillida. In their Peine de los Vientos (Wind Comb), a waterfront public space was transformed into a seaside park. His more recent España Industrial Park, in Barcelona, is an example of his work away from his region, and also away from his so well-understood natural context. In Barcelona, the relationship established between building and location does not achieve the same sensual, poetic dialogue as do his works in San Sebastián.

This deeply idiosyncratic architecture was inherited by some of Ganchegui's disciples: Miguel Garay and José Ignacio Linazasoro, most noticeably. Both have gained special relevance and recognition through their rethinking of public housing, and as the younger inheritors of the respect for local traditional architecture. Garay and Linazasoro's housing at Mendigorría from the 1970s is a good example of the employment of traditional construction techniques. Their professional careers have brought them to differing ideas and work priorities. Linazasoro's work continues to be respectful of context, as can be seen in his housing project of 1985 at Vergara, while Garay has incorporated a somewhat revisionist element in his later works (Casa de Cultura at Pasajes, 1985).

Several architects accompanied Garay in his eclectic enterprise. Iñiguez de Ozoño's housing at Getxo is an example of this new organic and detailed architecture. Javier Cenicacelaya and Iñigo Solaña can also be included in this generation of architects who, having inherited the idiosyncratic style of Linazasoro and Garay, believe that the past can only be surpassed by knowing and understanding it.

The architecture of Javier Vellés, although Basque, seems more cosmopolitan than that of his local colleagues, as proven by his "shadowhouse" in Cercedilla

72. Peña Ganchegui, España Industrial Park, Barcelona, 1986

(75), designed with María Luisa Sardá, or his more recent conference center built in Jerez de la Frontera, Cádiz, in the southwest corner of Spain (76). Also, the works of Fernando de Olabarría and Daniel Fullaondo in Bilbao are clear exceptions to this revisionist, contextualizing panorama.

Seville

Gabriel Ruiz Cabrero recently stated that Seville is fast becoming the third important architectural center in Spain. In his opinion, the new "Seville school" theoretical leader is Victor Pérez Escolano, who plays a similar role to that played by Oriol Bohigas in the Barcelona school.

Three historical moments have prepared the atmosphere for the creation of this School: the competition to build the Colegio de Arquitectos (West Andalusian Architecture Association); the housing program to remodel the Pino Montano area; and Expo 1992—the most recent opportunity for local architects to adapt the city to its growing needs.

The competition for the Colegio de Arquitectos was won by Gabriel Ruiz Cabrero and Enrique Perea, with a project that skilfully integrated rationalism, Andalusian culture, and Seville. While Seville is not the most rational city in Spain, the Ruiz Cabrero-Perea project achieved a

73. José Ignacio Linazasoro, housing, Vergara, 1985

perfect combination of respect, functionality, urbanism, and architectural value.

The housing program for the Pino Montano area was an ideal opportunity for local architects to demonstrate their skills, ideas, and ability to redefine local architecture within a new and modernized public housing program. Antonio Cruz and Antonio Ortiz were one of the first architecture teams to participate in the urbanization of the Pino Montano area. They proposed rectangular housing blocks with an interior patio derived from the Andalusian housing tradition. The buildings designed by Cruz/Ortiz have kept the very functional, severe line of the best Modern Movement examples, but are respectful of the Andalusian climate, tradition, and needs. Like that of Cruz and Ortiz, the projects of the Sierra brothers and Antonio Barrionuevo were functional, yet respectful of the Andalusian housing tradition and were fundamental in the development of the area. The projects designed for the Pino Montano area are some of the best work in recent Andalusian architecture.

Guillermo Vázquez Consuegra has translated the rationalist ideas he inherited and adapted them to his own cultural context. Mixing functional accuracy with rural traditions, his studio has produced some of the best examples in recent Andalusian architecture, such as his

public housing project in Ramón y Cajal Street *(78)*, Rolando house *(77)* in Mairena de Alijarafe, Seville, and their recent Sailing Pavilion for the Expo 1992. His work incorporates traditional Andalusian materials, spatial layouts, and colors, as well as the parts of the traditional regional house.

Antonio Cruz and Antonio Ortiz's Santa Justa Station in Seville was also designed as part of the Expo infrastructure. Recently finished, this simple but elegant project is the first building completed in the remodeling of a neglected area in the southern city. Rational in its spatial layout and use of geometric shapes, traditional in the employment of strong materials, this project is but one in the exemplary professional career of these two young architects, who have already produced other designs of interest. The best examples are their housing in María Coronel Street, and the Maritime Museum in Cádiz *(79)*, where a group of military buildings was converted into a series of covered galleries through a new juxtaposition of elements.

Valencia

ETSAV, the Valencia school of architecture, remained relatively unconsolidated while the two main architectural

74. Javier Cenicacelaya, Sagrada Familia School, Derio, 1990

76. Javier Vellés, conference center, Jerez de la Frontera, 1991

75. Javier Vélles/María Luisa Sardá, "shadowhouse," 1976

77. Vázquez Consuegra, Rolando house, Seville, 1983

teaching centers in Madrid and Barcelona were not only absorbing international avant-garde trends but also starting their own schools of thought. These autonomous movements were usually adaptations to local needs of imported tendencies, as well as foreign formal and philosophical ideas.

The Valencia school of architecture did not have a tradition of its own, unlike other schools in the country. Its professors had studied either in Madrid or Barcelona, and had learned the concepts and languages that were being developed there. Acknowledging this debt, the Valencia school has produced several architecture firms which, borrowing ideas from the international Modern Movement and its adaptation through the hands of some of the national architecture masters, like de la Sota and Coderch, have been able to rethink and adapt the Movement's principles. In Valencia it is common to find large groups of professionals working under a single name, producing a comprehensive architecture that includes buildings, interior design, furniture, and graphic design as well as landscape architecture. Together with such groups as Vetges tu i Mediterranea *(80, 81)*, and La Nave, other local studios like Carlos Salvadores, Emilio Jiménez, and Cristina Grau have developed a coherent local interpretation of the Modern Movement by bringing abstract international ideas to a more tangible popular stage.

78. Vázquez Consuegra, Ramón y Cajal housing, Seville, 1988

79. Cruz/Ortiz, Maritime Museum, Cádiz, 1988

80. Vetges tu i Mediterranea, Turia Garden, Valencia, 1990

81. Vetges tu i Mediterranea, Turia Gardens, Valencia, 1990

44

Conclusion

"The architecture systems of History were not a product of fantasy and caprice, but, rather, they express the essential character of a period and a region: social structure, construction techniques, proper materials, economic needs, spiritual demands."
—Editorial presentation in *AC-Documentos de Actividad Contemporánea,* periodical of the GATEPAC, no. 1, first quarter, 1931

A succinct analysis of the historic periods that characterized the beginnings of modernity in Spain will suffice to explain the late success of the Modern Movement, as well as the failure of postmodernism, which was never thought of as a movement or even as a group interest, and found only a few followers in the country. At the time when the Modern Movement was gaining international prominence and acceptance, it was difficult for Spain, a country isolated by force, to share its ideals.

On the other hand, the forty years of the Franco regime's "architectural watch" fulfilled the pre-postmodern quota of historic revisionisms. Hence, the Modern Movement has played a fundamental role in the most recent contemporary Spanish architecture, which progressed from modernity to a direct international connection with deconstructivism, largely ignoring the revisionist tendencies of historicism.

With such a wide and eclectic panorama, it has not been an easy task to select a group of architects whose work represents the tendencies of the best new architecture being produced in Spain. Besides the thirteen architectural firms presented in this book, some very interesting works, such as the hotel by Carles Ferrater in Barcelona *(82,83),* currently under construction, and Miguel Prada Poole's recent Palenque in Seville, part of the Expo 1992 infrastructure, deserve special mention. Although Ferrater has been most frequently classified with other Catalan architects of his generation, his work has lately been departing from the very discreet, even respectable, lines followed by many other architects and is moving toward a more personal concept and increasingly risky, more original, spatial layouts. In his new hotel's floor plans, constructivist concepts are used as references, instead of his previous restatements of established local trends.

As discussed in the context of the 1970s, Prada Poole *(84,85)* is still very active—supporting emerging technologies and quasi-utopian ideas for a new architecture. Fitted with a mechanical artificial cloud and rain system, his Palenque, recently finished in Seville, aims to become a refreshing oasis in the middle of the Expo, which is scheduled to open in the summer of 1992.

While the work of Piñón and Viaplana *(86),* as well as that of Navarro Baldeweeg *(87),* must be recognized and mentioned in any book dealing with contemporary Spanish architecture, the author has chosen to publish instead the work of less-known, younger architects, whose formal expression and conceptual framework has evolved from the influence of these established masters.

This book is a synopsis of contemporary Spanish architecture from 1986 until September 1991, when the manuscript was closed. The architects whose work is featured here represent, indeed, The New Spanish Architecture.

T H E
ARCHITECTS

ALFREDO ARRIBAS

Louie Vega Discothèque • Calafell • Tarragona • 1988

Alfredo Arribas is a maverick in Barcelona's architecture scene. An extremely creative architect, he is better known for his flamboyant interiors and industrially produced furniture designs than for his very accurate, correct, respectful, and yet thoughtfully innovative architecture. He has become a very fashionable architect and a reputed designer, due to his interiors for many well-known restaurants, bars, and night clubs. He was one of the first designers in Catalonia to reevaluate modernism and its use of organic images and traditional materials. Strangely enough, his work is modern, functionalist-based architecture, with historical and local references. In many of his early commissions, he looked for a theme (cinema, the Masonic world, a ship sinking, etc.), which he developed to an unbelievable extreme. When designing new buildings, his attention to detail is reflected in the innovative and rationally organic shapes of the supporting structure, in the cubic plans, and in the project's final outcome, which very rationally serves its expected function, like his warehouse, or his more playful Louie Vega Discothèque. Arribas has proved to be a rational architect—searching for new ways of expression, new ways of thinking about architecture. An examination of his designed details and use of materials shows very little improvisation, coincidence, or aspects left to chance. A closer look at his floor plans confirms the rationale underlying the visual and sensitive game of his architecture.

A complex program of shifting uses organized this project. A separate building was designed for each of the planned activities: dancing, drinking, cloak room, entrance hall, toilets, etc. These pavilions were connected by a

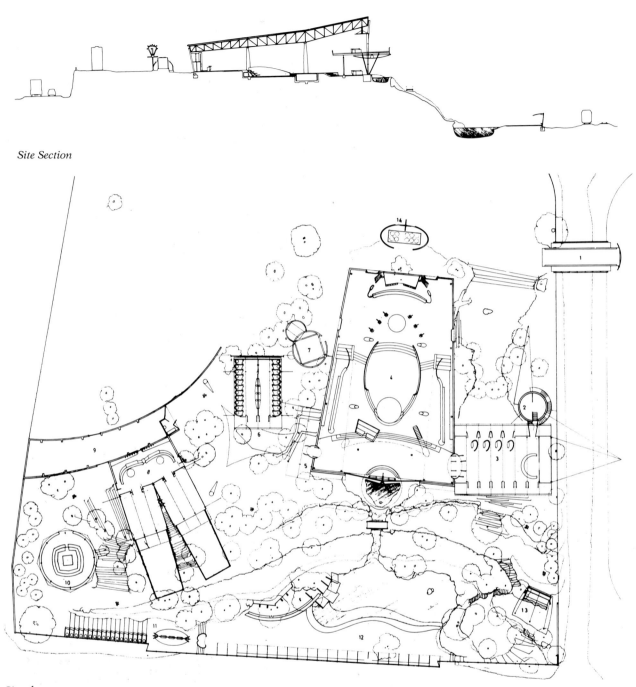

Site Section

Site plan

central corridor that serves as the access area and unifies the project with a literary theme that evolves from pavilion to pavilion.

The particular location of the project, between the sea and the railway tracks, and the fact that there was only a six-month period to complete both design and construction, were key factors in determining the layout and materials used in this project. The Louie Vega Discothèque received the prestigious FAD architecture prize.

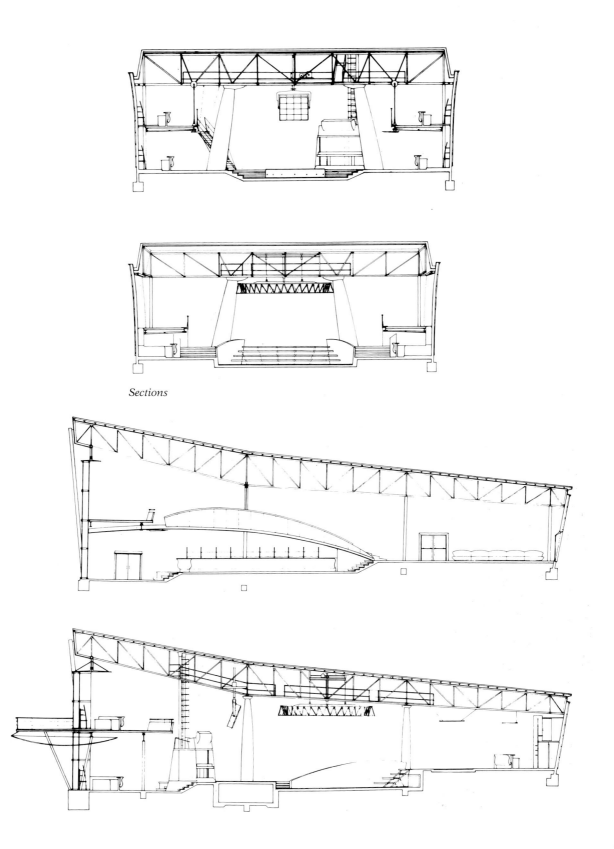

Sections

Warehouse • Mercabarna • Barcelona • 1990

Located in a storage and industrial area on the outskirts of Barcelona, the building is an empty space designed for maximum storage capacity and wholesale commerce. It is composed of three different, integrated enclosed volumes: refrigerators, offices, and a service core. The various details of its functional structure were also designed by the Arribas team.

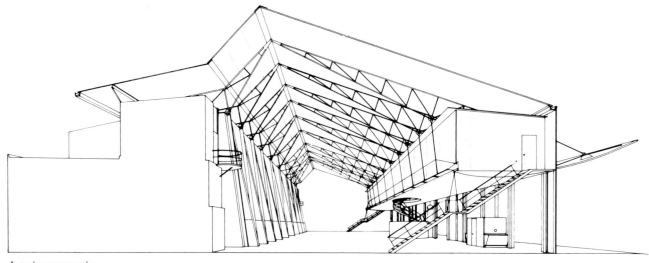

Interior perspective

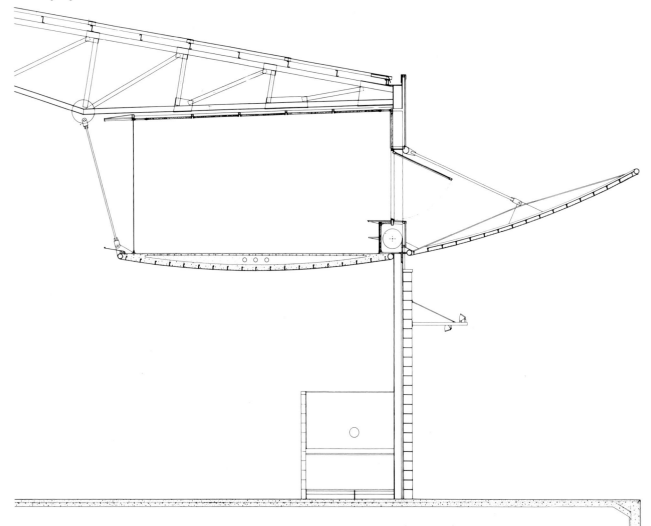

Wall section

58 ALFREDO ARRIBAS

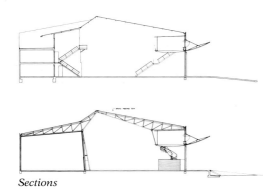

Sections

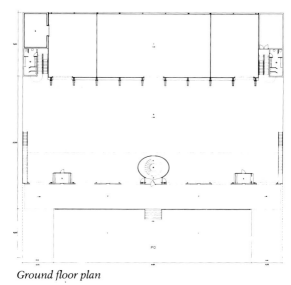

Ground floor plan

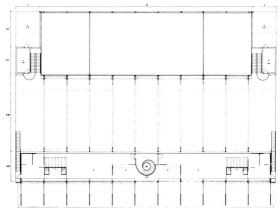

Second floor plan

Marugame Office Building • Takamatsu • Japan • 1991–

This oval-plan building is located in a sculpture park, and is intended to become its largest piece. The new building interacts with the square where it is located and the surrounding art pieces through a constant play of shadows.

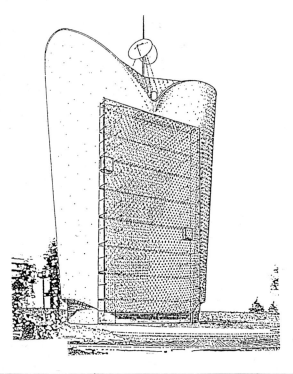

Site Plan
1- Canopy with grids covering the car park
2- Truck pavilion
3- Kitchen
4- Restaurant open to the square

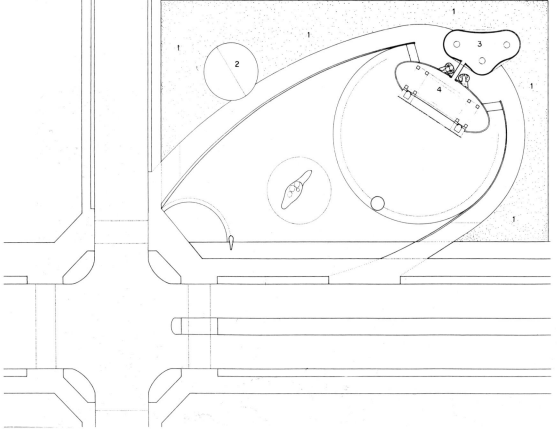

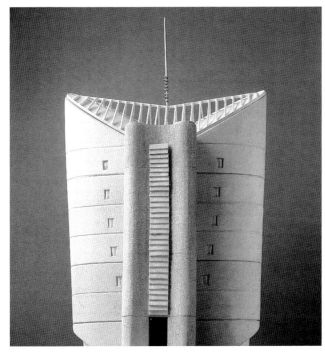

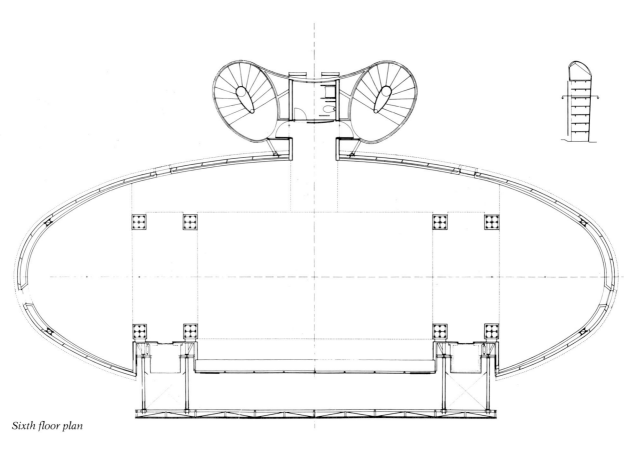

Sixth floor plan

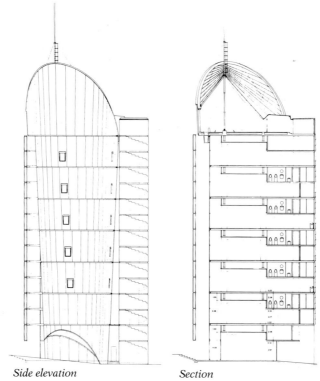

Side elevation   *Section*

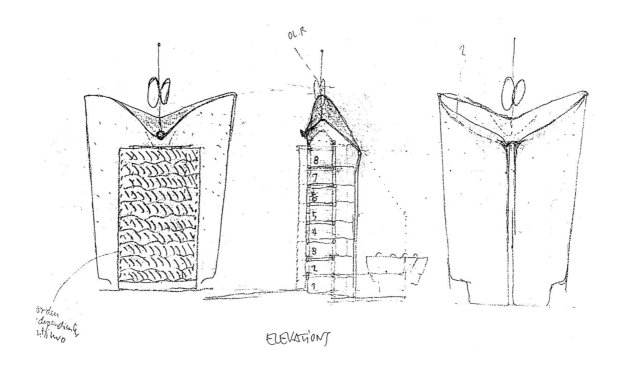

ELEVATION

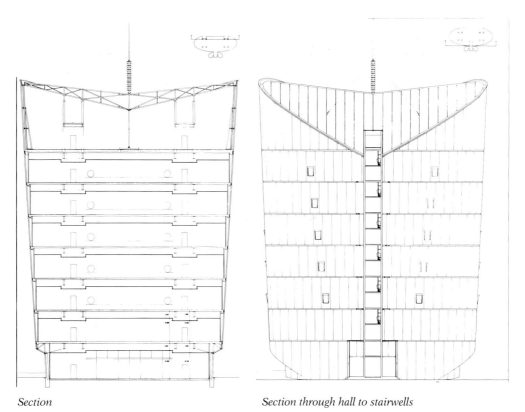

Section   *Section through hall to stairwells*

IÑAKI AVALOS/JUAN HERREROS

Waste Water Treatment Plants • Majadahonda • Madrid • 1990

Iñaki Avalos and Juan Herreros are both instructors at ETSAM, the Madrid school of architecture. In addition to their professional practice, they have also contributed to many architecture publications and have lectured on contemporary problems and issues facing architecture, such as the reorganization of the modern city, skyscrapers, and the need for a new building which can adapt to new needs.

Although they recognize the debt of contemporary architecture to the Modern Movement, Avalos and Herreros realize the need to improve, update and re-evaluate the Movement's basic tenets. They believe that the Modern Movement should be re-examined and reconsidered according to the current needs of society and also according to the present advantages and possibilities new technology can offer. These professionals believe contemporary architecture should be planned from the general to the particular and very strongly support the construction of sky-scrapers, believing that the verticalization of the city is a necessary step toward better urban planning and, therefore, better living. As seen in their competition-win-ning proposal for the new head-quarters of Telefónica, these architects are capable of producing a resourceful, functional, and original architecture that radically differentiates their work from an easy re-creation of that of the Modern Movement.

The treatment plants are basically composed of a bypass valve and the two other systems it connects: a man-made treatment element and natural river waters. These functions involve different types of engineering and require interventions of considerable scale on the topography, creating

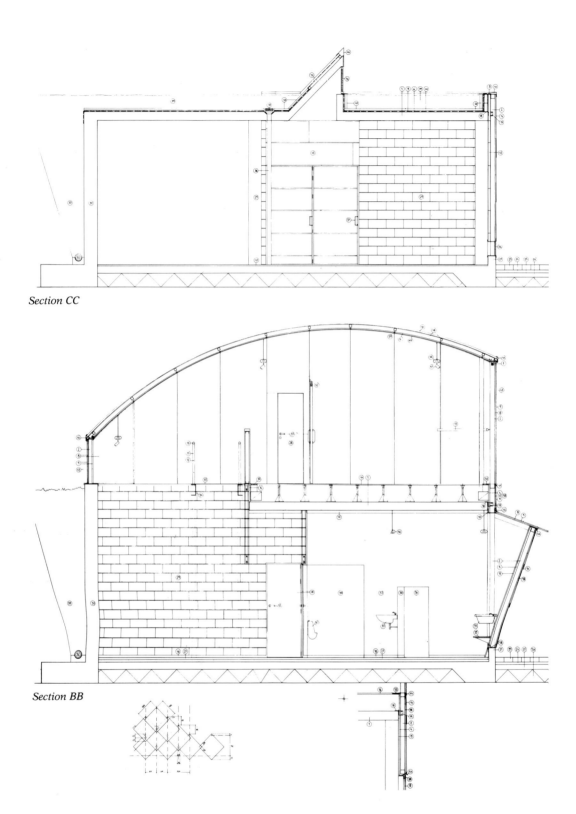

Section CC

Section BB

artificial platforms beneath which the successive treatment processes are half buried. Equipment containers, silos, control and service buildings contribute through their layout to the ordering of this process, and are executed with almost didactic simplicity. Through the materials used, "cold" (such as aluminum, zinc plates, and steel for the outside) and "warm" (plywood board on the inside), and the spatial layout, the final image is intended to evoke a technical garden.

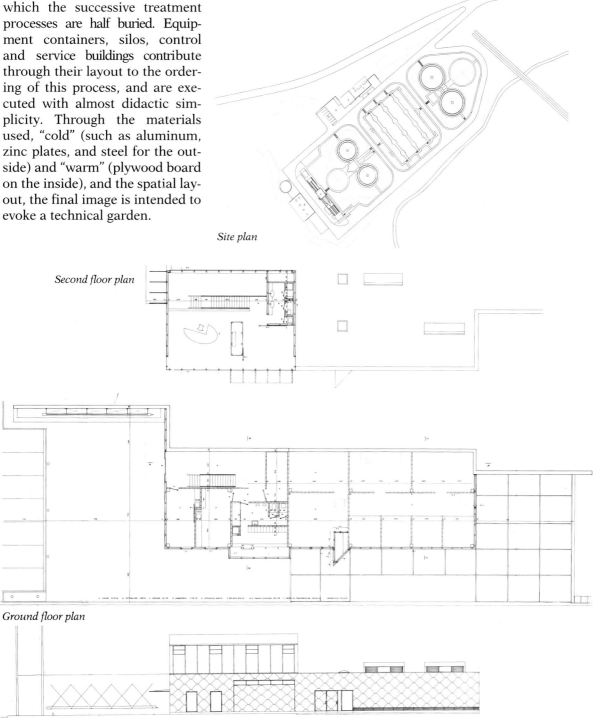

Site plan

Second floor plan

Ground floor plan

Elevation

Multiuse Gymnasium • Simancas • Madrid • 1991

The commission was to design a sports center that could also be used for large meetings in a historic rural area. Economy of means was the key to the precise design that confronts both the river and the old city. Consisting of a large, translucent, perfect box, the building was designed to become an abstraction of its intended function. Prefabricated lightweight trusses support the flat roof structure.

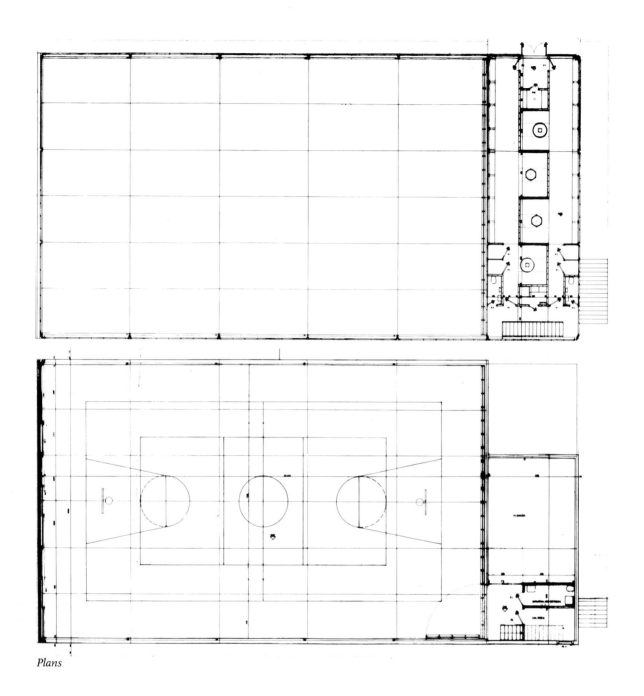

Plans

Sections

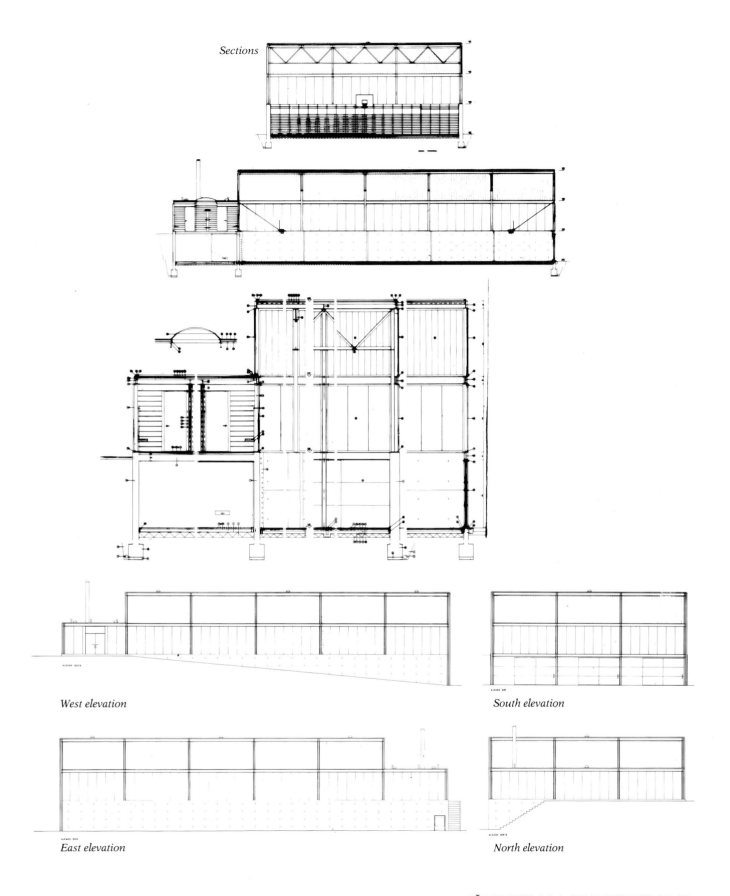

West elevation

South elevation

East elevation

North elevation

Housing at the M-30 Motorway • Madrid • 1991–

Located by the M-30 Motorway, which surrounds Madrid, this project is part of a housing program in which several reputed architects have been invited to participate. Contrary to most of the built projects that tried to isolate the dwellings from the motorway, that of Avalos and Herreros is a large open space facing the motorway where an intense traffic show takes place.

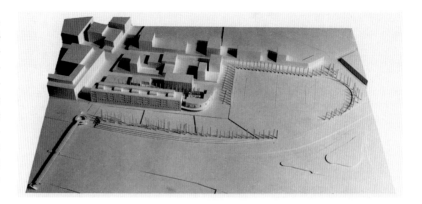

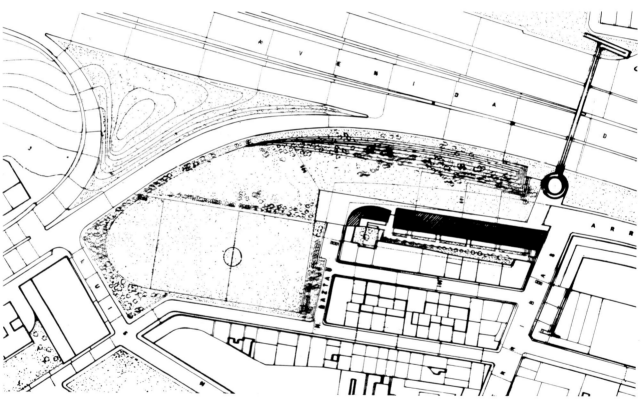

Site plan

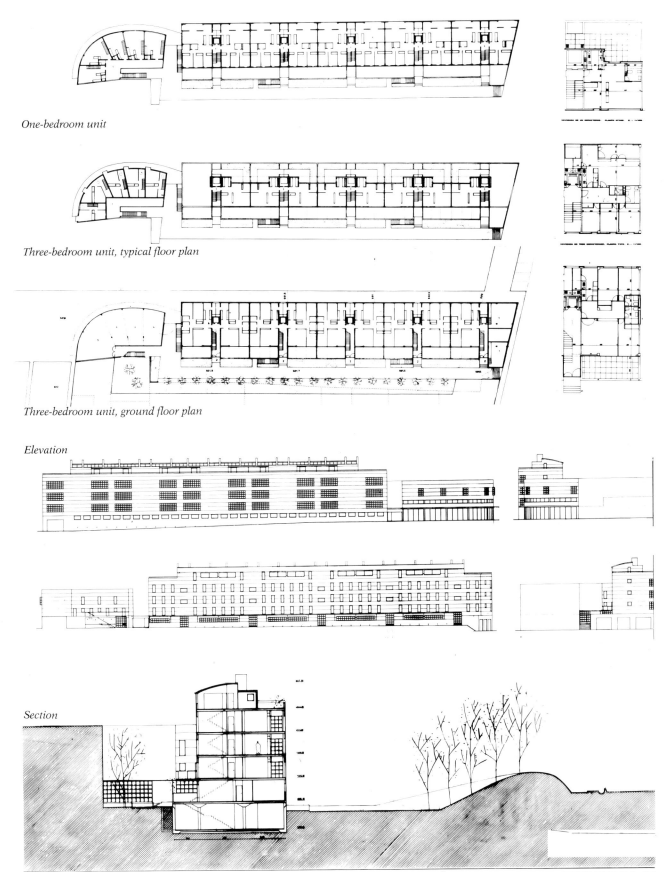

One-bedroom unit

Three-bedroom unit, typical floor plan

Three-bedroom unit, ground floor plan

Elevation

Section

ENRIC BATLLE & JOAN ROIG

Bridge on the Besos River • Sant Adriá • Barcelona • 1989

Batlle and Roig both worked in the Martínez, Lapeña and Torres studio—probably the strongest influence and reference for their projects' spatial layout, plasticity, and exquisite, yet simple, details. Other strong influences come from the Catalan school of the late 1970s and early 1980s, and some of their abstractions and more conceptual work can be traced back to that of Piñón and Viaplana. Respectful of the landscape, they believe in nonintrusive architecture that continues and adapts to nature rather than opposing it. Because of this, they have won several competitions to build parks inside the city of Barcelona and in its surrounding areas. Among their best nationally known projects is the cemetery on the slopes of the Collcerola Mountains in Barcelona, where architecture and landscape fit perfectly.

The cross section of the bridge is asymmetrical, stepping down toward the sea. Three different radii of curvature govern each of the bridge's three platforms: the lowest one works as a pedestrian promenade, while the central platform is assigned to vehicular traffic. The highest platform, narrower and farther away, and also intended for pedestrians, protects the rest of the bridge from the visual aggressivity of the nearby power lines. Because of these changes in elevation, the bridge appears varied and fragmented, while, at the same time, it acquires its own character as an urban space. Like gigantic crutches, the piles support the bridge's nonchalant randomness in a strict and rigid manner.

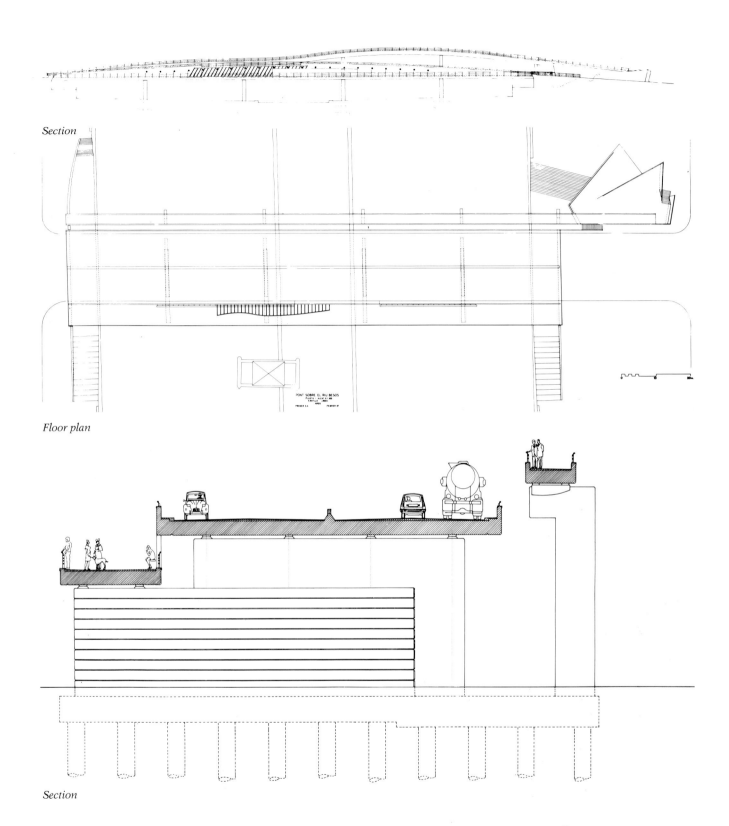

Section

Floor plan

Section

Zinnia Flower Shop • Barcelona • 1991

A series of stepped marble platforms, with a constant section but a complex geometry, unifies the space, materializing in a homogeneous support for the flower containers. It is the abstraction of an imaginary landscape, placed under a ceiling with a spherical dome. Under this virtual sky, this tectonic image multiplies in the mirrors above, and becomes visible beyond the shop windows.

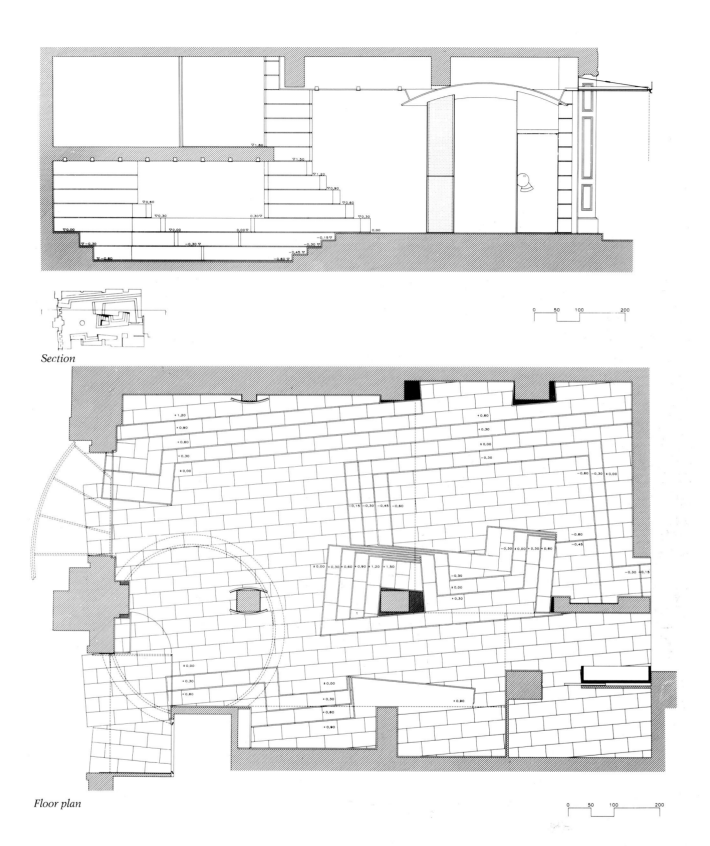

Section

Floor plan

Fontes Palace • Murcia • 1991

To rehabilitate the palace, the additions that had been built on to the old baroque structure on Fontes Square were demolished. A new, free-standing building was erected, with a multilevel courtyard separating the new from the old. From the courtyard, a palm tree looks out on the Azucaque alley. The new building maintains the palace's former alignments, and is constituted of a black stone plinth, a solid body covered with stucco and with small, randomly located punch openings, and an upper loggia with a copper roof.

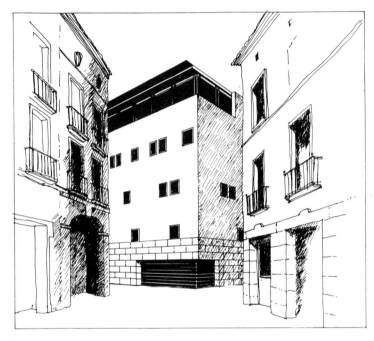

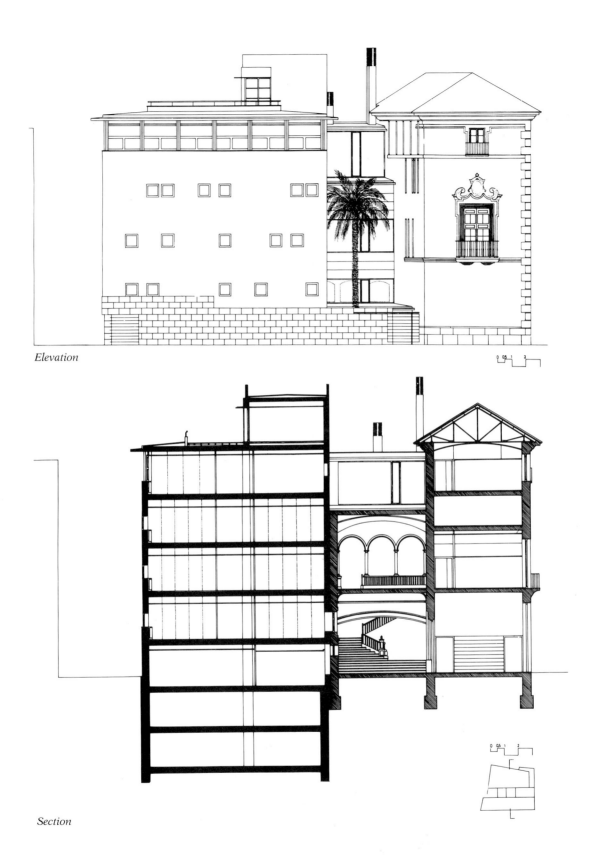

Elevation

Section

ENRIC BATLLE & JOAN ROIG   85

ENRIC BATLLE & JOAN ROIG

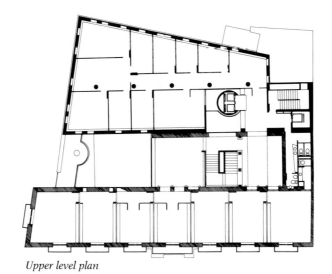

Upper level plan

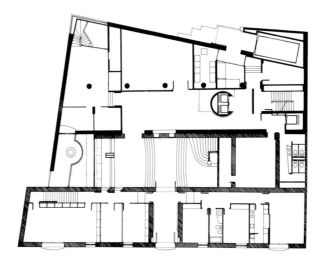

Middle level plan

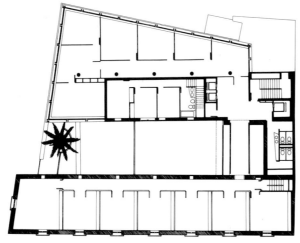

Lower level plan

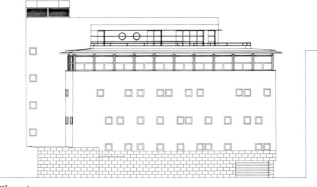

Elevation

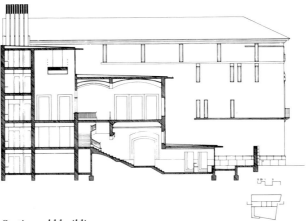

Section, old building

Section, new building

SANTIAGO CALATRAVA

Bach De Roda Bridge • Barcelona • 1984–87

Section

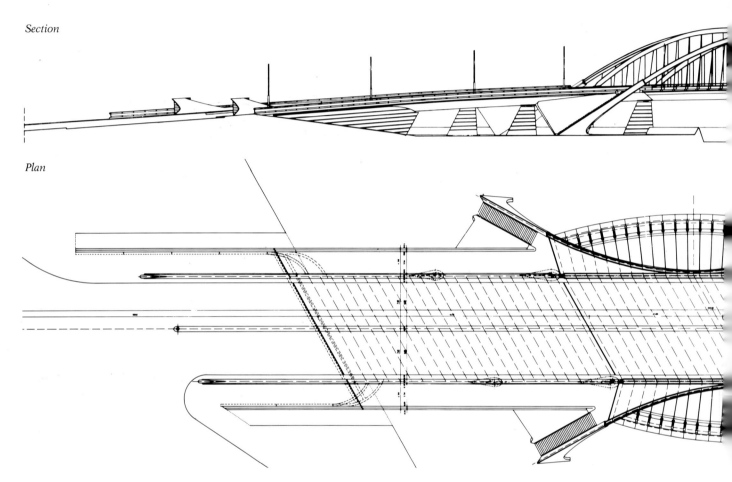

Plan

Calatrava's constructions, especially his bridges, are often mistaken for sculptures, identifiable as objects with their own character and disposition. Juxtaposed to, or rather imposed on the geographical context, Calatrava's architectural elements become landmarks, monumental art pieces produced by a recognizable author.

Santiago Calatrava is an atypical architect. Trapped between the plastic arts and engineering, the Valencian archi-

tect conducts the three professions at once through a single object. He imagines his pieces like an artist, designs them as an engineer, and builds them like an architect. In spite of his education, he claims his is a self-taught working system, and he acknowledges that travel has been an important aspect of his training as an architect.

Calatrava's use of state-of-the-art technology, folding structures, solid materials, and aerodynamic shapes, his interest in

breaking barriers, in provocation, in the search for new spatial organizations and compositional styles, his utopian, almost visionary, character and his commitment to introducing a new vocabulary of soft forms, in tune with the spirit of the times, have brought him to the forefront of international architecture.

It may be difficult to appreciate that Calatrava's architecture is truly international, and that the relationships it estab-

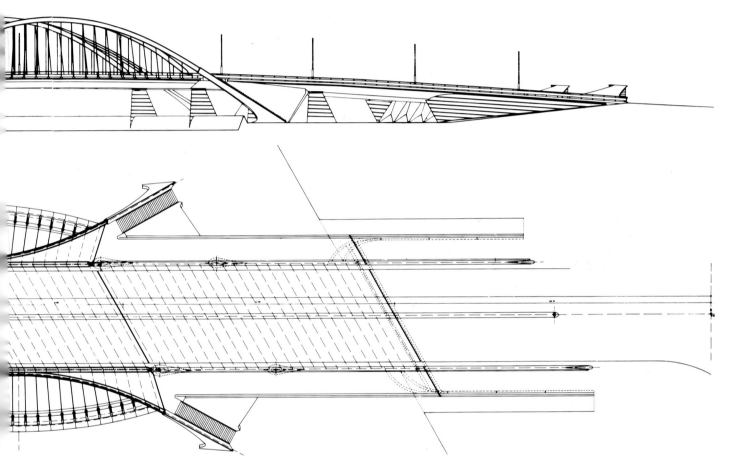

lishes with its different contexts have more to do with volumes, sizes, and spaces than with the particular cultures found in the various regions in which his structures are located. Santiago Calatrava is also one of the few Spanish architects who sees the computer as an essential tool in the evolution of the architectural profession, for its perfect suitability for organizing the modular, repetitive systems that are integral to any work.

The bridge, both link and gateway, spans the railway tracks between two main streets which run from north to south, connecting the sea and the city. The twin arches widen slightly at both ends, increasing structural rigidity and permitting the passage of pedestrians on footpaths located on both sides. Steps follow the line of the arches on both sides of the railway. The road lights are located on the center band of the bridge, while the footpaths are lit by strip lighting integrated into handrails.

Bilbao Airport • Bilbao • 1990– (under construction)

An important aspect of the conception of the airport for Bilbao, in northern Spain, is the views perceived by users arriving either by motor vehicle or aircraft. The airport is comprised of a large hall for all flight procedures, and wings housing the waiting and access areas to the planes. The steel and concrete structure is carefully integrated into the hilly, green landscape.

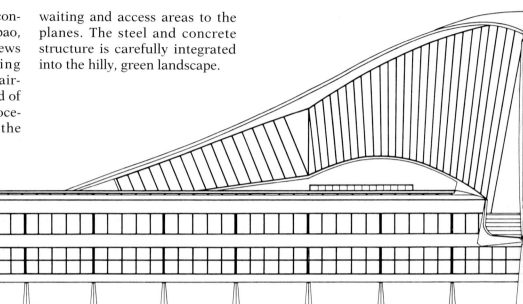

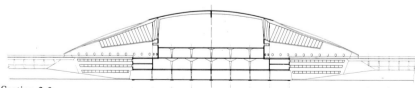

South elevation

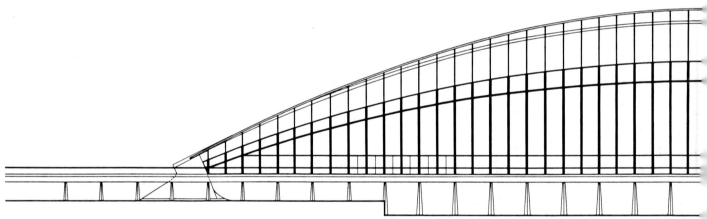

North elevation

Section 2-2

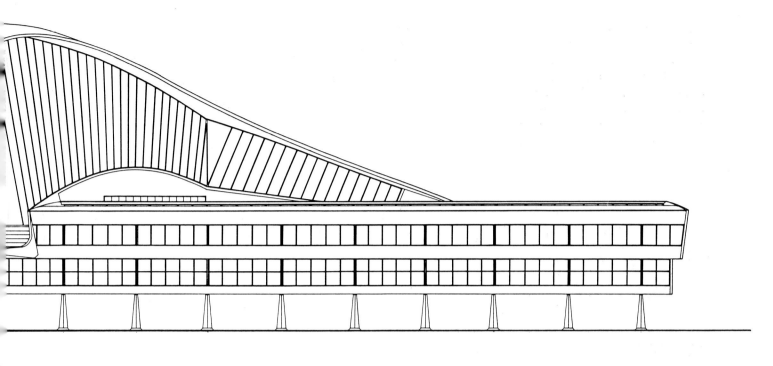

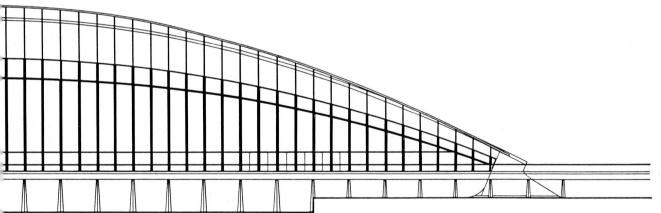

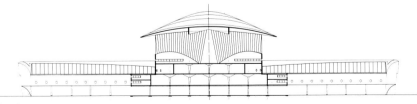

Section 3-3

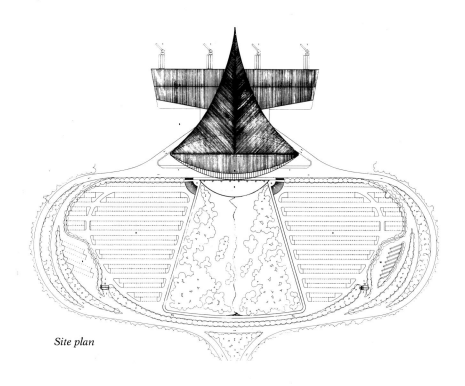

Site plan

Section 1-1

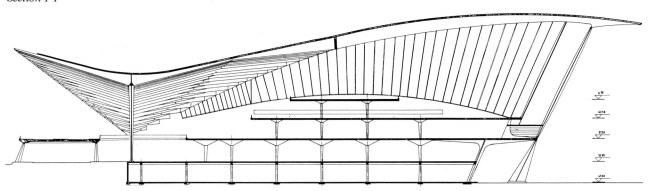

West elevation

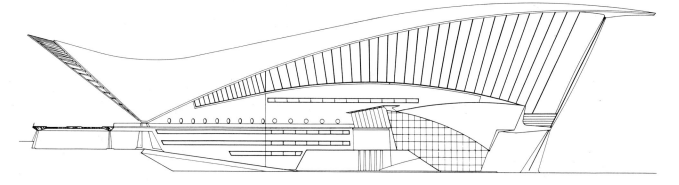

96   SANTIAGO CALATRAVA

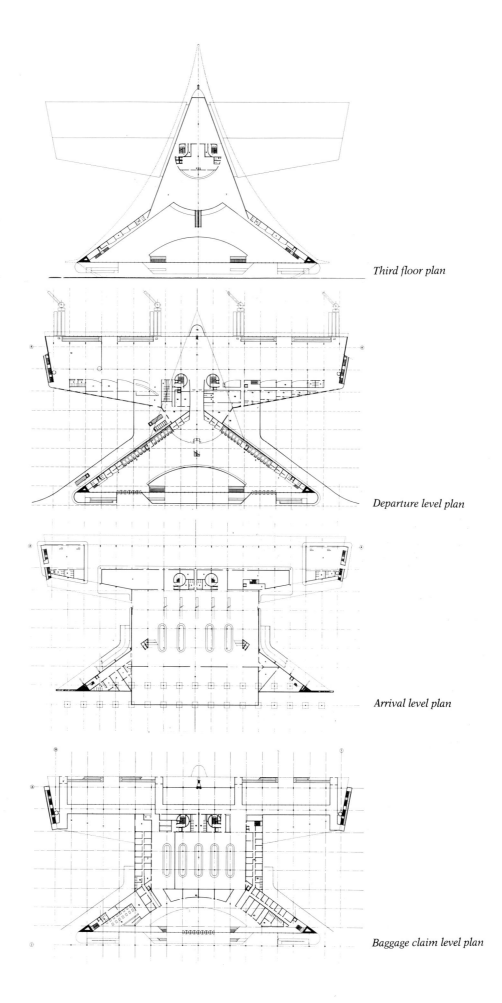

Third floor plan

Departure level plan

Arrival level plan

Baggage claim level plan

Extension, Stadelhofen Railway Station • Zurich, Switzerland • 1984–91

As part of the local railway network, Stadelhofen Station must accommodate the heavy traffic increase expected in the next few years. Therefore, a third track is being added, along with an adjacent trackless platform. The main structural components are the protective wall, which is set back from the platforms, the gallery which covers the railway on the side nearest the mountain, the newly erected bridge connections, and a retail level which acts as an underpass to the intermediate track. The duality of the mountain and the valley, which arises from the positioning of the railway line, is emphasized by the structural elements in between, with light steel bridges connecting both areas. The remaining elements of the station, the roofs above the tracks and the canopies are organized to convey the greatest possible unity.

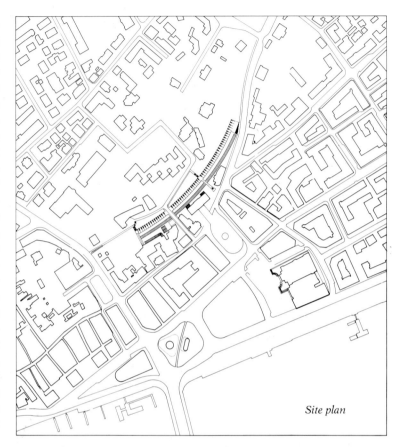

Site plan

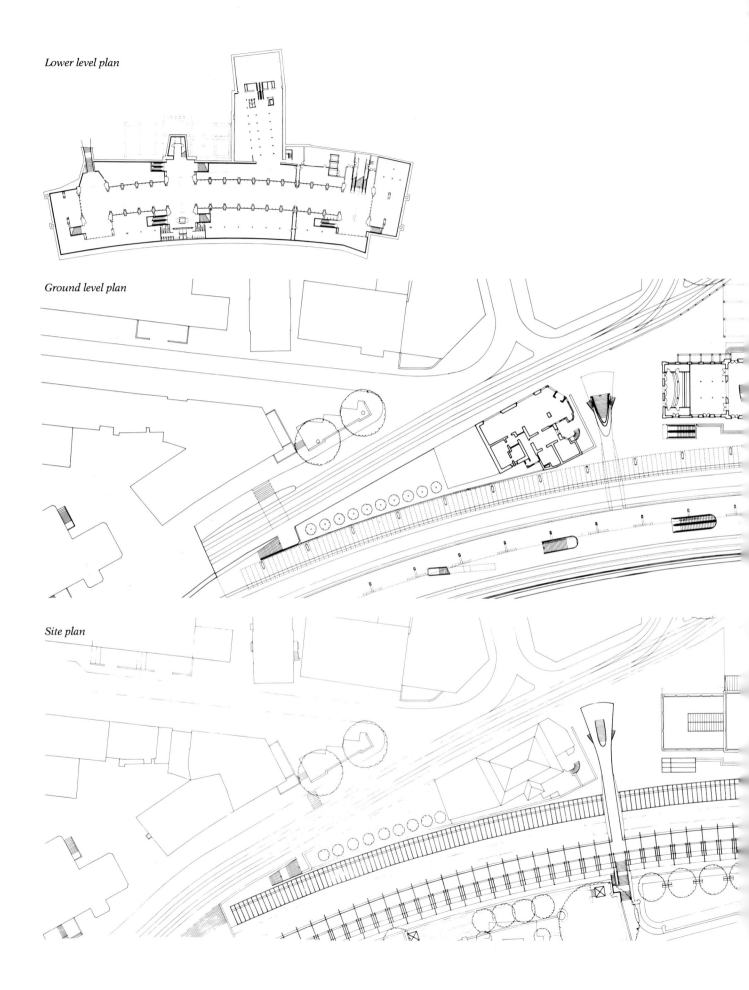

Lower level plan

Ground level plan

Site plan

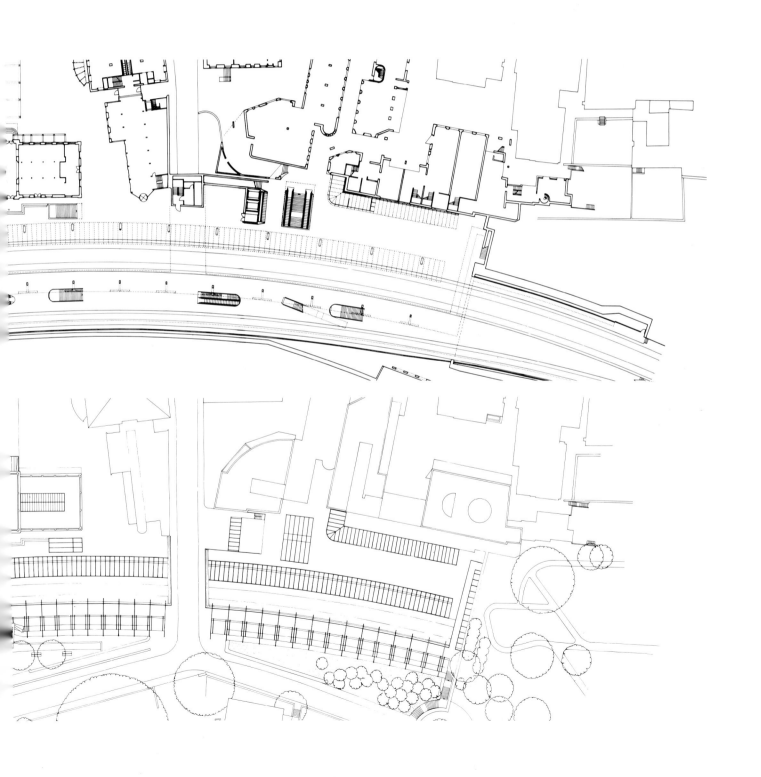

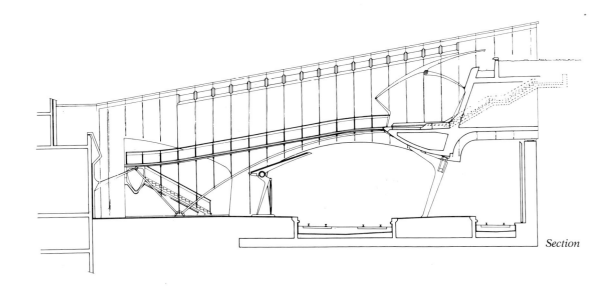

Section

Section

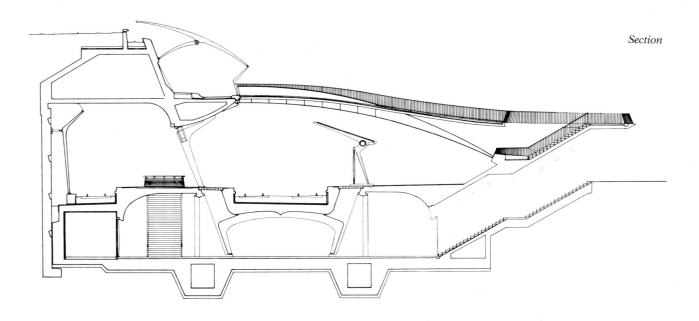

ALBERTO CAMPO BAEZA

Turégano House • Pozuelo • Madrid • 1987

Alberto Campo Baeza designs modern, uncomplicated, affordable architecture. His buildings share the same simplicity, careful natural illumination, and perfect geometric volumes. Other than the context, which is likely to be rural, only the client, be it a poet, a painter, an average family, a town hall, or a diplomat, sets the differential key which establishes conceptual variations of his simple schemes.

Campo Baeza's architecture, economic both in cost and in means, could be applied more logically and coherently to public housing. In this field, far from being accused of using Modern Movement ideals without improving its historic mistakes, or being questioned for building bourgeois houses with the Movement's language, Campo Baeza's challenge is to demonstrate a new and successful application of the old principles.

The Turégano house is the project that best reflects Campo Baeza's architectural ideals: simple and pure rigor, strict functionalism, and strong International Style influences.

The house is adapted to the sharp slope of the land plot where it was built, between the

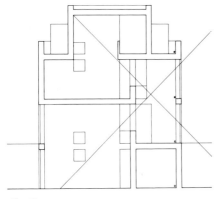

Section

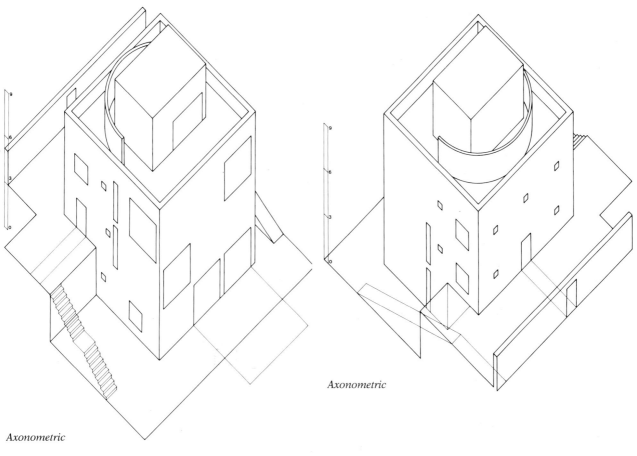

Axonometric

Axonometric

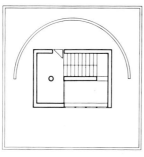

Top level plan

Middle level plan

Entry level plan

Lower level plan

access from the street and the garden/playing area. The house, a strict, cubical, tense construction, opens to the south and the garden, while closing to the north façade that confronts the street. The interior has been resolved through the creation of two-story spaces that intercommunicate diagonally with the main rooms of the home. Light plays a special role, becoming almost a theme, by illuminating the interior either directly or by reflecting on all the white surfaces.

Gaspar House · Zahora · Cádiz · 1991

The high, thick, white walls protect the house from the sun, while wide openings allow light in the interior. The Gaspar house, surrounded by two patios that double its rectangular size, is yet another example of simplicity brought to the limit by almost entirely avoiding interior partitions.

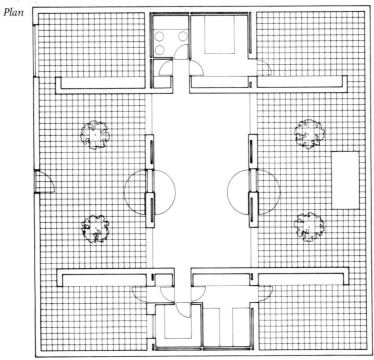

Plan

Drago Public School • Cádiz • 1991

Following the Miesian rule "less is more," which Campo Baeza has adopted and adapted to "more with less," this public school facing the ocean in Cádiz, the southeasternmost point in Spain, is another example of the architect's simple functionalist work and understanding of the International Style. The building, a perfect geometric figure with a wide opening to allow light inside, also exemplifies Campo's obsession with light. The interior is organized around a central patio that allows natural light in each classroom.

JOSE MANUEL GALLEGO JORRETO

Cultural House • Chantada • 1990

Jose Manuel Gallego Jorreto was born in Galicia in the mid-thirties. He studied architecture in Madrid, where he worked for Alejandro de la Sota, also from Galicia. From his experience with this architectural master, he inherited great respect for the basic rules of the International Style and functional architecture. After completing his doctoral dissertation, Gallego returned to his homeland, an agriculture-based area, and started studying the evolution of the rural architecture of the region. He published several essays on the subject of "Rural Architecture and Landscape" (1974), and on "Landscape Formalization" (1977), and started addressing this theoretical concern in his own work. He applied the rationale he had learned from de la Sota, during a time when many architects were designing in a more organic style, to his own culture and landscape. Therefore, his architecture, although clearly indebted to the International Style, is not international, but local, very much tied to the idiosyncrasies, materials, traditions, and culture of the Galician region at the northwest of the Spanish peninsula. This profound link to the landscape, regional materials, culture, and tradition is much more visible in this region than in any other part of Spain. The reason for this is likely to be found in both the very extreme weather and geography of the area and the fact that it still remains rather isolated and more idiosyncratic than other areas in Spain. In this respect, Gallego's architecture can be given credit for taking modernism one step further, humanizing it, and adapting it to particular needs. His is not an international but a local reading of the Modern Movement´s theories.

This project undertook the rehabilitation and remodeling of an old house. The existing neglected building had to be kept due to its importance in the local urban context. The building's exterior was simply restored with very minor modifications, and it was literally "hung," like a picture, on a new supporting wall. The interior was drastically transformed into a unified, unique space.

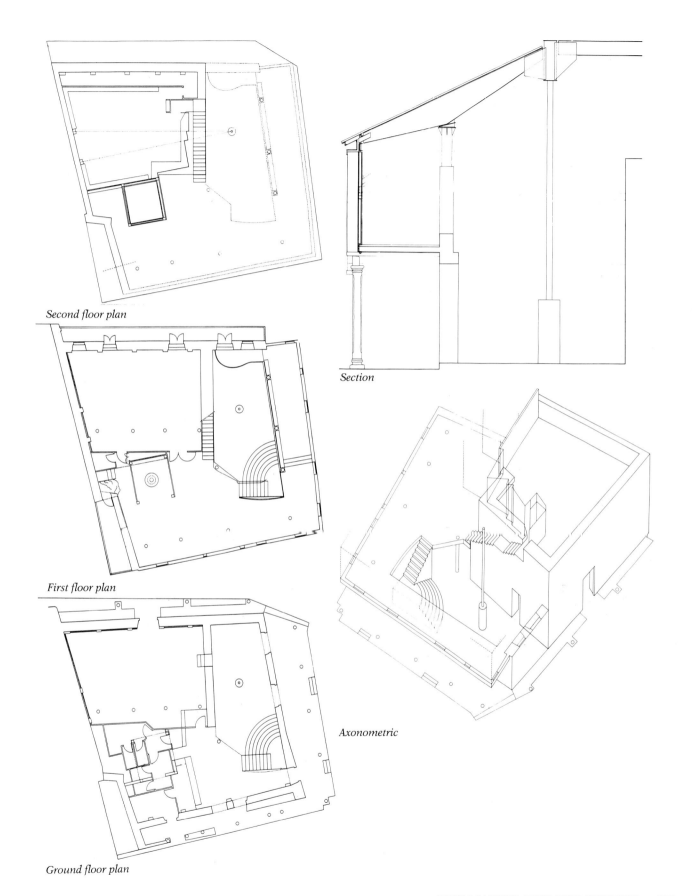

Second floor plan

Section

First floor plan

Axonometric

Ground floor plan

JOSE MANUEL GALLEGO JORRETO   121

Cultural Center • Valdoviño • 1991

Located in a rural area, the building was intended to reorganize the neglected urban structure of Valdoviño. The old road to the village was also repaired at the same time the cultural center was built, achieving a total transformation and restructuring of the rural area through a new, public urban space.

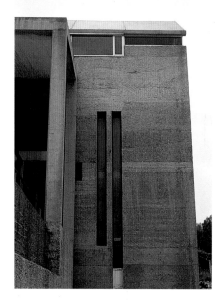

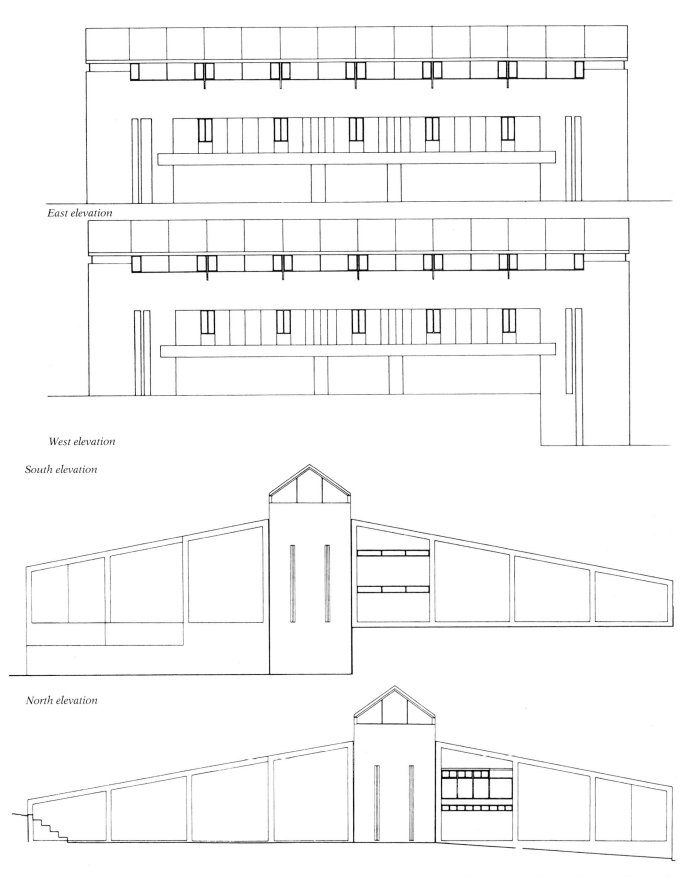

East elevation

West elevation

South elevation

North elevation

JOSE MANUEL GALLEGO JORRETO   123

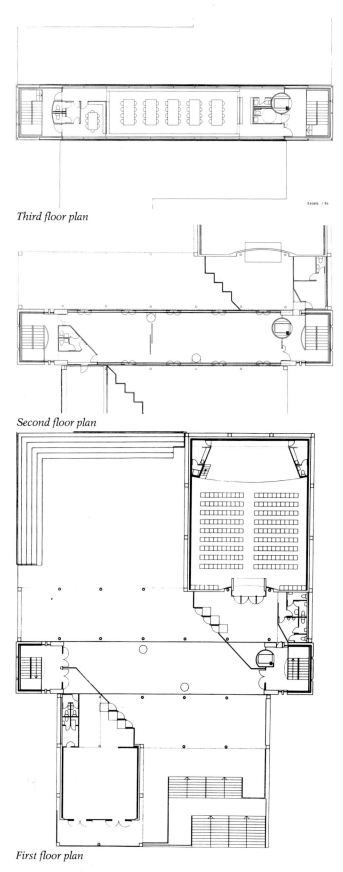

Third floor plan

Escala 1 50

Second floor plan

First floor plan

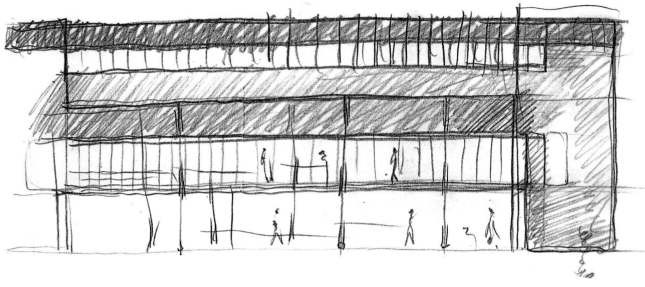

Housing at Montecelo • La Coruña • 1987–91

The ability to design a public housing project well is, in the opinion of many architectural critics, what defines a good architect. This project for fifteen houses in a rural area held a special appeal for Gallego, and he undertook serious studies of both private and common spaces within a community. Although the final result was not as he originally envisioned, due to disagreements with the client, the project develops a new way of ordering and organizing collective housing: volumes or flexible space containers left unfinished to be completed by the dwellers.

Because of the above-mentioned disagreement, the housing at Montecelo is not Gallego's most representative project. Due to the comparatively small attention public housing has been given in the contemporary Spanish architecture panorama, this project, however, deserves special attention, since it represents a new solution to an old, and in many ways still unresolved, problem. Each circle in the floor plans represents a tree, to be chosen by the dweller, which would both separate the houses from each other and reinforce privacy and ownership of the land and house.

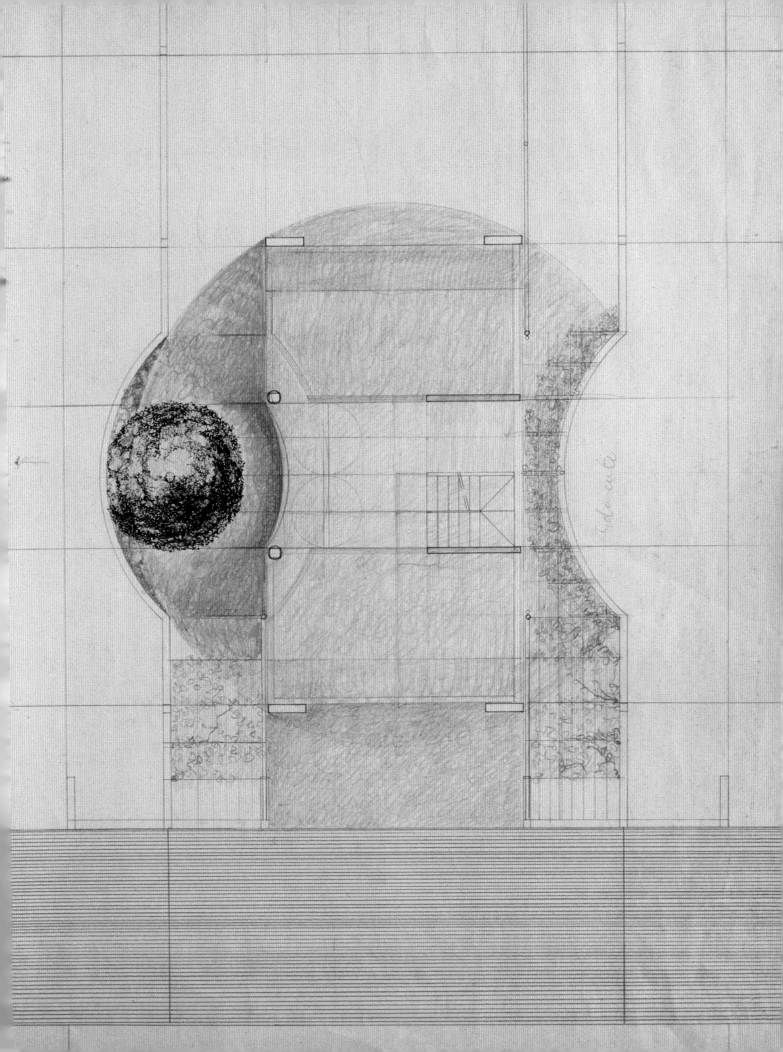

Section

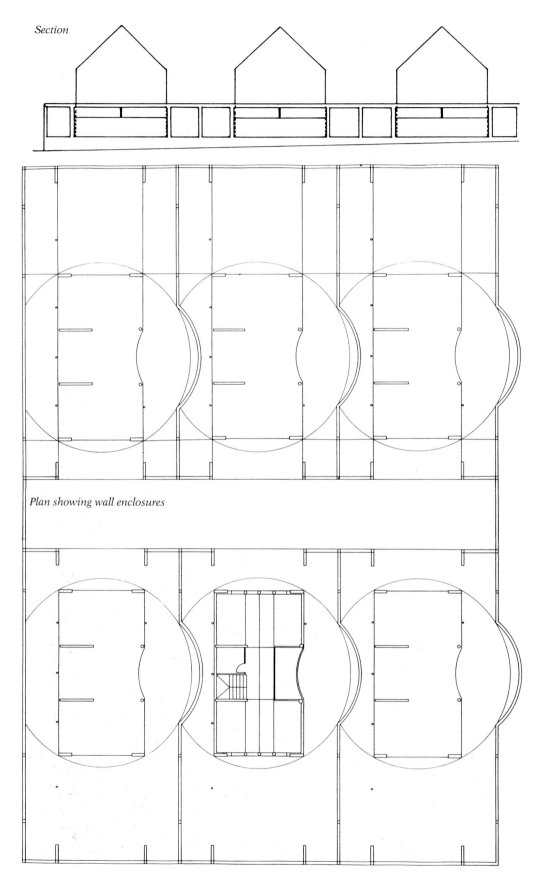

Plan showing wall enclosures

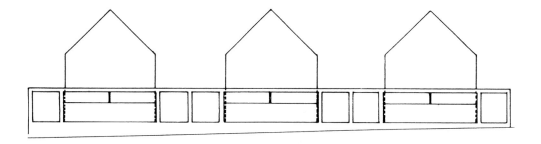

JOSEP LLINAS

Remodeling of the Archaeological Museum • Barcelona • 1989

Josep Llinás's work summarizes the collision between the radical, severe rationalism in the 1950s and 1960s by people like Alejandro de la Sota, and the correct, clean, discreet architecture that followed the emergence of the so-called school of Barcelona.

Llinás's architecture is deferential to its context, establishing, however, more of a dialogue than an opposition or continuation of the context, whether urban or rural. His formal expression uses very simple geometries, recognizable typologies, severe architecture, almost reaching the purist radicalism of the shapes in Piñón and Viaplana's latest works, but establishes, however, a different relationship with the surroundings. With careful spatial layouts, detailed finishes, simple elements, and a strong geometric basis, Llinás's is a very simple and elegant architecture. Although it cannot be said to have altered architecture's evolution by improving its relationship with the individual, by using new construction materials, or by introducing a new way of ordering space, Llinás has tried to find his own way among trends and stronger currents with an architecture that employs the basic rule of "simple is beautiful." The tasteful selection of materials transforms this otherwise simply correct architecture into very special buildings.

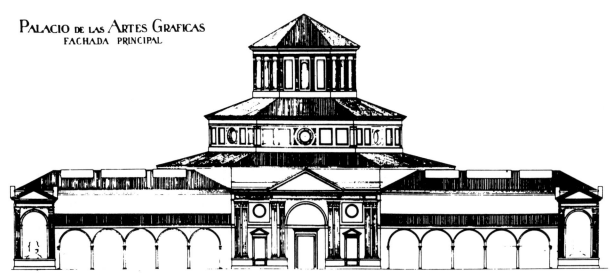

Elevation (archival)

Ground floor plan (archival)

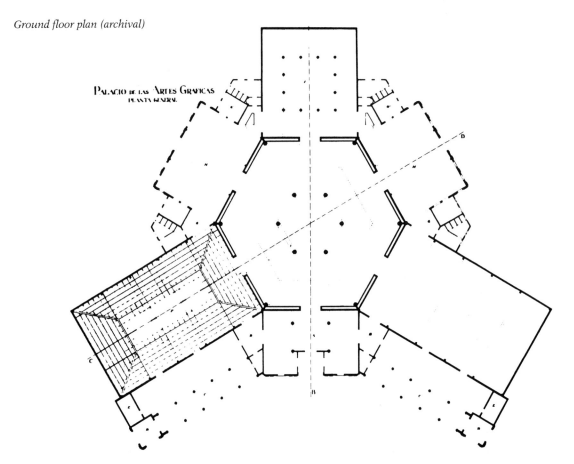

The spacial layout of the original 1929 building consisted of several rectangular galleries surrounding a central hexagonal core. The remodeling project refurbished the central room, establishing a new entrance hall with direct access to all the galleries. Further alterations are planned to complete the building's rejuvenation.

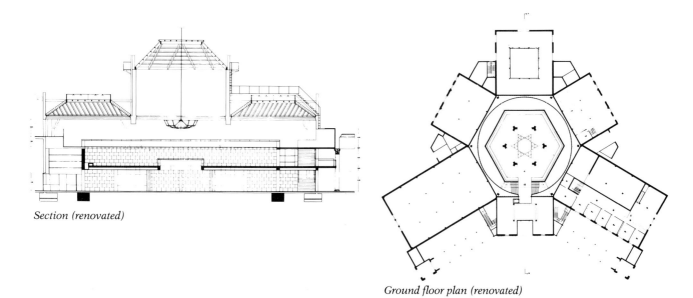

Section (renovated)

Ground floor plan (renovated)

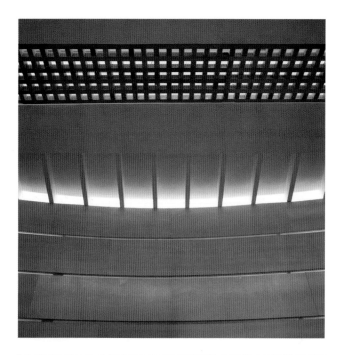

Apartment and Office Building • Vilafranca del Penedés • Barcelona • 1990

Having been commissioned to design a multiuse building in Vilafranca, a town near Barcelona, Josep Llinás was faced with several problems regarding the unusual site, surrounded by very small and eclectic structures, on which the building was to be built, and the tight budget. The façade was to be built using prefabricated sandwich panels made of treated sheet metal and filled with expanded polyurethane. During construction, however, at a point when the structure was finished and the floor slabs were ready to receive the sandwich panel enclosures, the owners requested that conventional construction systems be used for the enclosure, for economic reasons. The building was then "dressed" with stucco, marked with an arbitrary masonry bond pattern, stretching from the attic to the sidewalk. The stucco borrowed its colors from the neighboring buildings to further enhance the building's adaptation to a context that, other than in color and size, is randomly eclectic.

Seventh floor plan

Sixth floor plan

Fifth floor plan

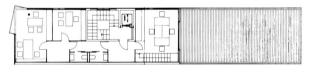

Fourth floor plan

Third floor plan

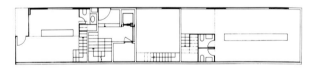

Second floor plan

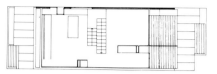

First floor plan

Elevations

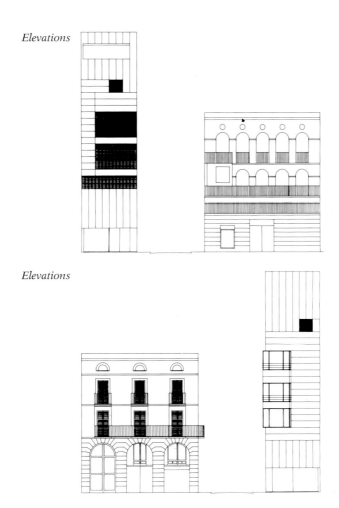

Elevations

Restoration of Theater Jujol • Tarragona • 1991– (under construction)

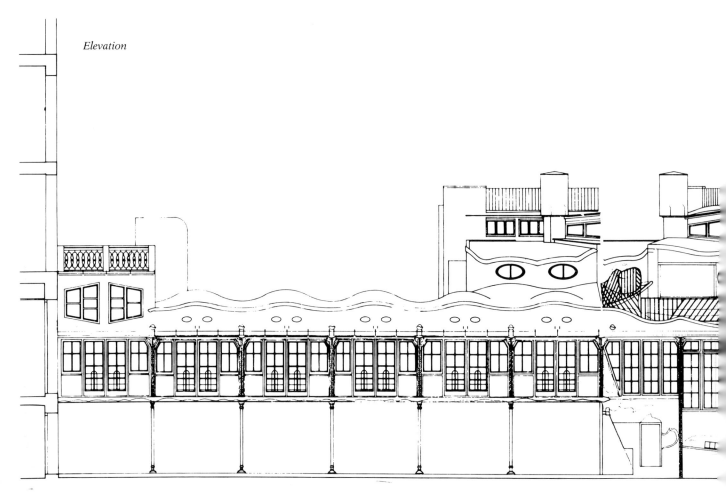

Elevation

The theater, which was designed by the modernist architect Josep María Jujol, had been neglected for many years. During the Spanish Civil War it was hit by a bomb, and the ensuing reconstruction was not especially respectful of the original design but, rather, simply attempted to repair the great physical losses the building had suffered. The building was eventually abandoned when the theater closed, and Llinás found it in a very neglected and ruinous state when he was commissioned to restore it. The restoration implied not only the transformation of the existing structure into a modern theater, but also the restoration of Jujol's building, which considerably increased the complexity of the project since no original drawings were available. Comprehensive research on the ornamentation of the building had to be undertaken. After very thorough study, naval and marine motifs were chosen as fundamental references in the refurbishment of the building.

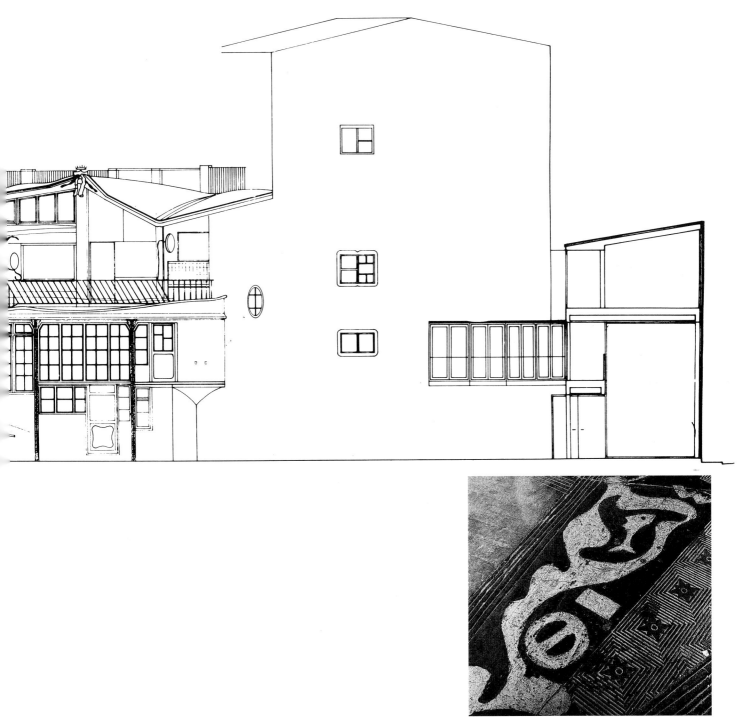

Section   *Ground floor plan*

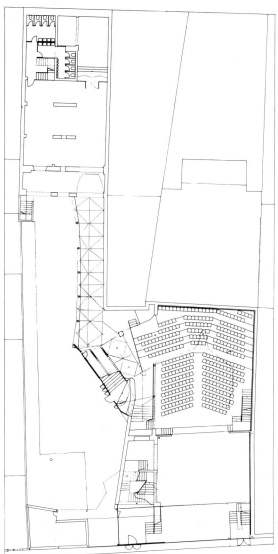

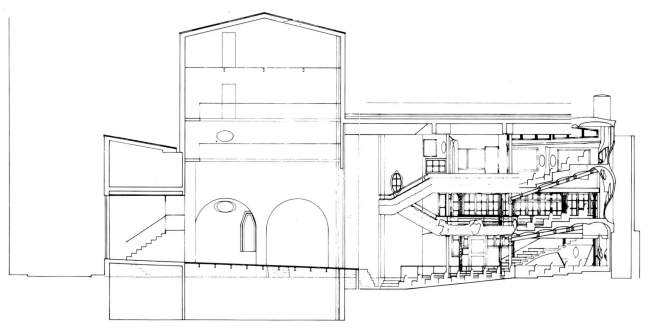

Section   *Balcony level plan*

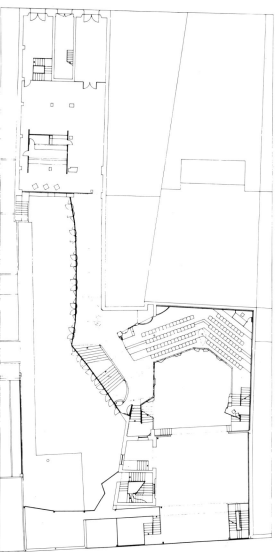

JOSE ANTONIO MARTINEZ LAPEÑA & ELIAS TORRES

House in Cap Martinet • Ibiza • 1987

Jose Antonio Martínez Lapeña and Elías Torres are an unlikely couple but a perfect match. Martínez Lapeña is a rational, accurate perfectionist with a down-to-earth spirit and is also introverted and reserved. Torres is the necessary counterpoint: vivacious, gifted with a very clever sense of creativity, extroverted, flamboyant, imaginative and yet very refined. Without the two of them, the work would probably not combine with such skillful mastery precise detail with playful atmosphere, elegant refinement with exquisite humor, and pragmatic function-ality with playful composition.

The influence of the Catalan master Josep María Coderch is apparent in their floor plans, coupled with a revaluation of the traditional Mediterranean architecture reconverted to their own plasticity. Another strong influence comes from the modernist Josep María Jujol. These two influences have been combined into a perfect symbiosis by the team Martínez Lapeña/Torres. This combination, added to their complementary tastes and skills, has resulted in a personal formal language, gifted with perpetual freshness, and is extremely convincing in its blend of precision, pragmatic detail, plastic idiom, and simple, yet elaborated, composition and character.

They seem to have learned the cubic and splayed geometry, space flow, and plasticity from Coderch, while the horizontality of their work can be traced back to Asplund, Aalto, or Wright. Torres and Lapeña, now in their late forties, while not internationally recognized, are an example and inspiration to younger Spanish architects.Torres and Lapeña are admired architects, and it is very clear that some members of the younger generation also included in this book (Batlle and Roig, Vendrell, Tarrasó, Marcos Viader, Val) who worked in their studio clearly learned their lessons.

The yellow and white colors of Josep Lluis Sert's house across the street are reflected in the entry façade of this house. To the east and south, the house views fragments of landscape while it tries to hide from its neighbors. The floor plan escapes the linear perimeter dictated by the zoning code through compulsive movements of the house's walls.

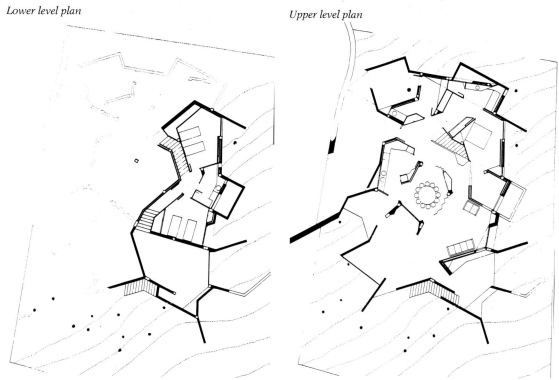

Lower level plan   *Upper level plan*

146   JOSE ANTONIO MARTINEZ LAPEÑA & ELIAS TORRES

Restoration Scheme for the City Walls • Palma • Mallorca • 1990–91
(with J. Henrich and O. Tarrasó)

The project was a MOPU (Ministry of Urbanism and Public Works) commission intended to transform the *Ronda* (sentry walk) into a long, linear park that will work as a terrace of the city overlooking the sea. Each separate area received special treatment. The project was a very detailed exercise, combining parks, stairs, gardens, ramps, open-air theaters, paving, and playing areas.

Folly Pavilion • Expo 90 • Osaka, Japan • 1990 (with Tosikazu Ishida)

Martínez Lapeña and Torres were commissioned to build a pavilion for the Osaka Expo of 1990. They were interested in working on the idea of how men have incorporated gardens into architecture. Their proposal was the construction of four objects, each one showing a different relationship between gardens and architecture. It was an animated construction in which, every fifteen minutes, one of the four objects displayed its mechanisms and, once every hour, all objects moved at the sound of the clock.

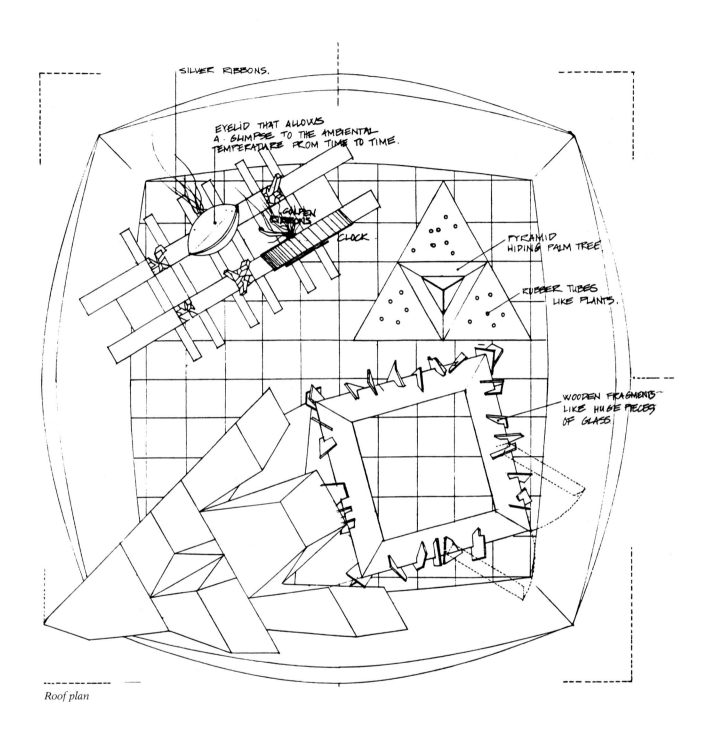

SILVER RIBBONS.

EYELID THAT ALLOWS
A GLIMPSE TO THE AMBIENTAL
TEMPERATURE FROM TIME TO TIME.

GOLDEN
RIBBONS

CLOCK.

PYRAMID
HIDING PALM TREE.

RUBBER TUBES
LIKE PLANTS.

WOODEN FRAGMENTS
LIKE HUGE PIECES
OF GLASS.

Roof plan

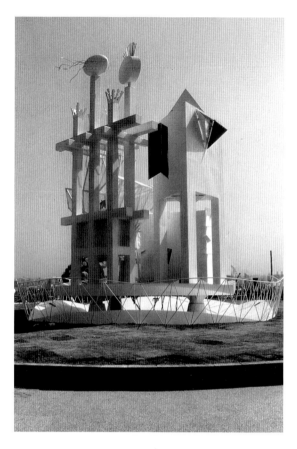

ENRIC MIRALLES/CARME PINOS

Hostalets Civic Center • Hostalets • 1989–91

As stated in *Architectural Review,* Enric Miralles "draws lines on paper that represent architecture, and he draws only slightly more substantial lines in space that are architecture."

In Pinós and Miralles's work, the circulation system acts as a basic determinant in the sequencing of spaces and in the fracturing of plastic forms. Ramps are a major compositional element in their architecture, which helps create new perspectives. Perception is, indeed, extremely important in the dynamic architecture of these two very young professionals, in which motion acts as the unifying factor.

Before joining his partner, Miralles had worked for Piñón and Viaplana. The Sants Square underlines the departure point from which both teams started their own architectural paths. Piñón and Viaplana moved toward forms of radically pure geometry, while Miralles and Pinós led their work toward the search for more radical forms of experimentation with irregular shapes, and opened their minds to the deconstructivist ideas shared by the international avant-garde.

Miralles and Pinós's work recognizes the talent, importance, and influence of the so-called deconstructivist movement. However, unlike the studios of Zaha Hadid or Coop Himmelblau, the Spanish architects' intervention in the existing context is not intrusive, but rather communicative. Although clearly visible, their manipulation of the setting is smooth rather than aggressive, and also modest, austere, respectful, and economical, while innovative beyond modernity. Their very young studio will have to prove, in the coming years, that they

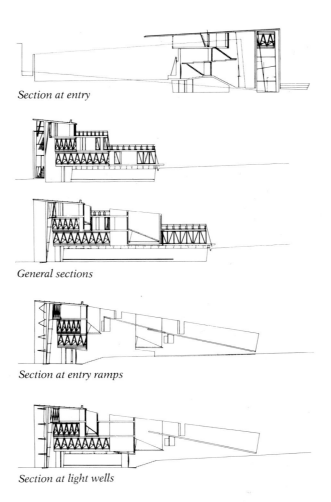

Section at entry

General sections

Section at entry ramps

Section at light wells

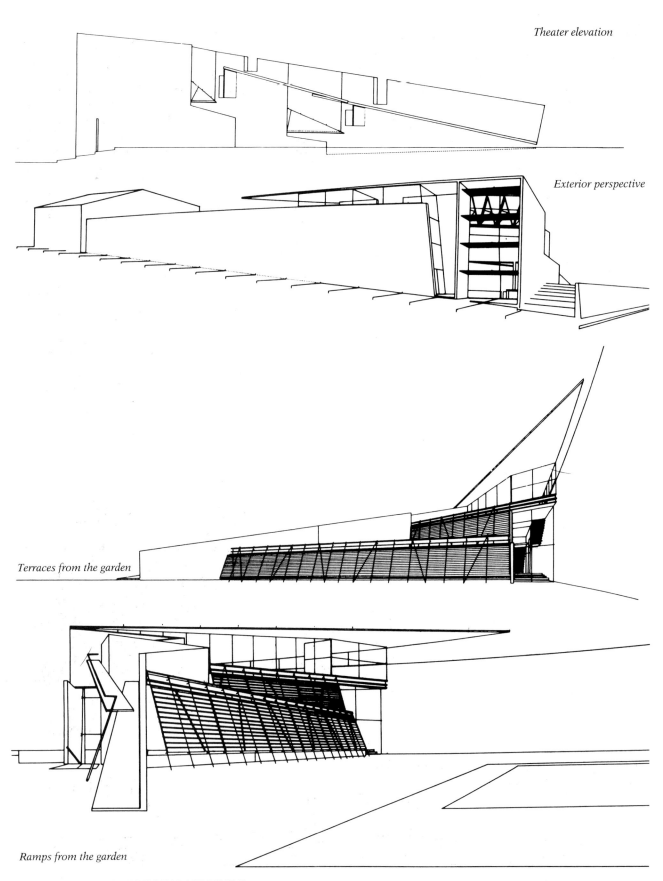

Theater elevation

Exterior perspective

Terraces from the garden

Ramps from the garden

162   ENRIC MIRALLES/CARME PINOS

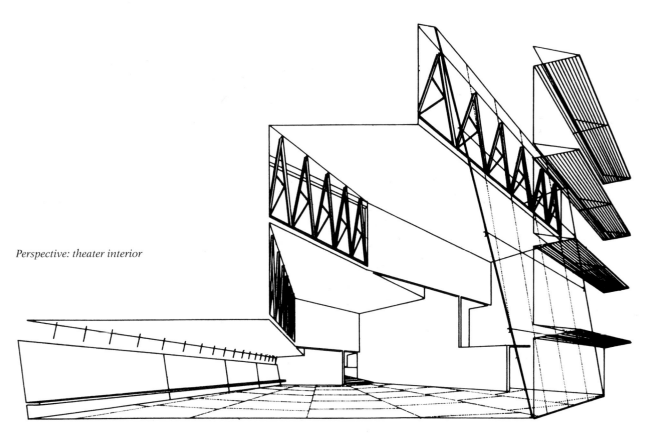

Perspective: theater interior

Cemetery • Igualada • 1991
(with Se Duch)

The architecture of Miralles and Pinós has been described as drawings with volume. Their manipulation of the context and their very particular way of respecting the program gives motion to their projects. The cemetery in Igualada is not only a place for the dead. The niches and tombs move forward and backward. The doors are mobile X-shaped figures, the paving is made of wood instead of concrete, and its integration and understanding of nature is such that the old dead leaves not only will not disturb the global image, but, rather, they will add to it.

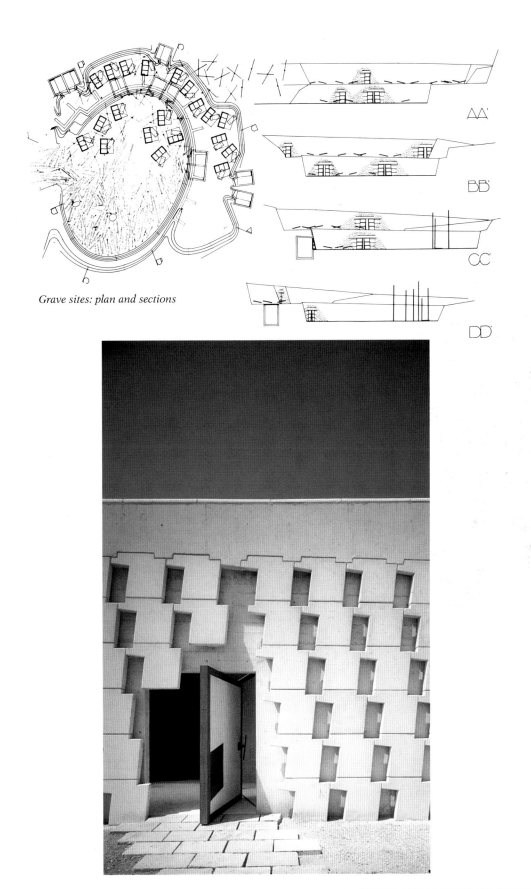

Grave sites: plan and sections

AA'

BB'

CC'

DD'

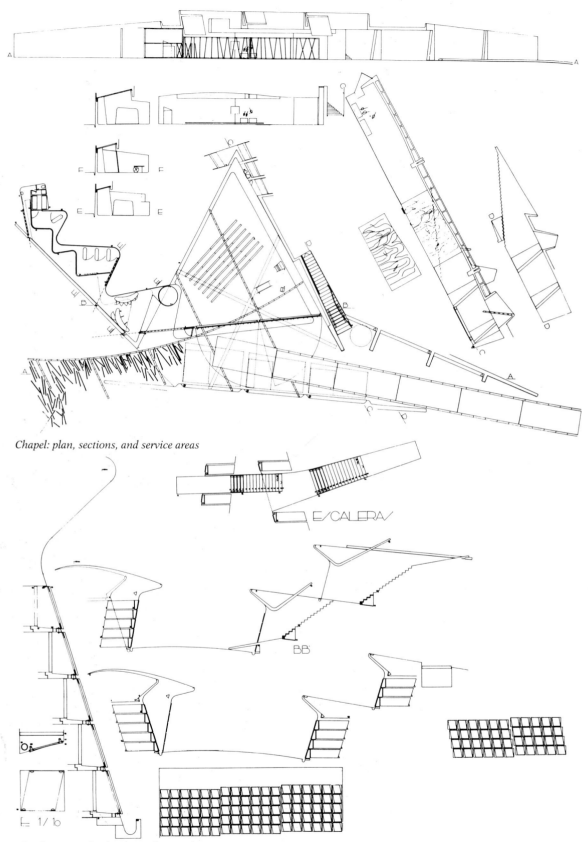

Chapel: plan, sections, and service areas

ESCALERA/

BB

E 1/ 10

Section: crypts and excavated covered passage

Archery Fields • Barcelona • 1989–91

The location of this project is conditioned by the earth slope on which it is built. The shape is the result of its retaining wall function coupled with the requirements for archery training and competition. The various folds of the training building are intended to be reminiscent of the athletes' movements. This project, according to its authors, "is not a matter of drawing, but simply of tracing." The final result is an interesting and respectful manipulation of the environment.

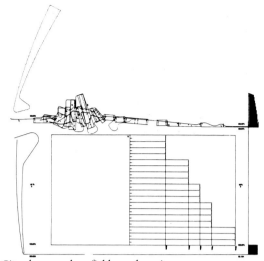

Site plan: porches, fields, and services

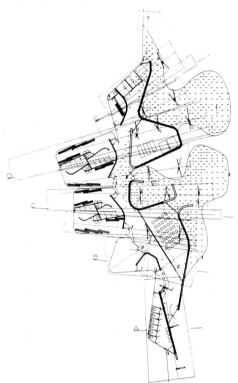

Changing facility corridor and public rooms

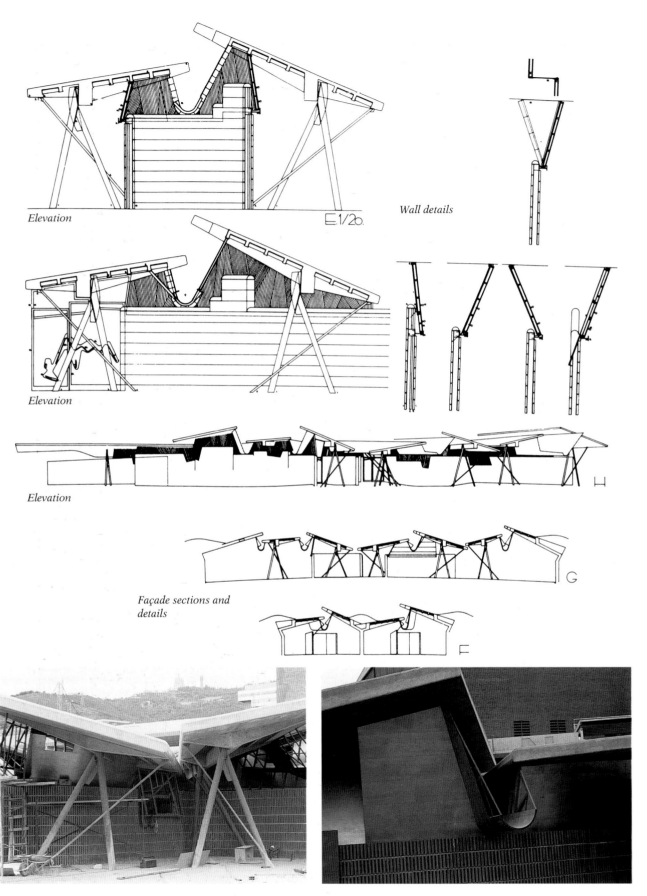

Elevation

E.1/20.

Wall details

Elevation

Elevation

Façade sections and details

G

F

RAFAEL MONEO

*Kursaal Auditorium • San Sebastián • 1990
(with Luis Rojo)*

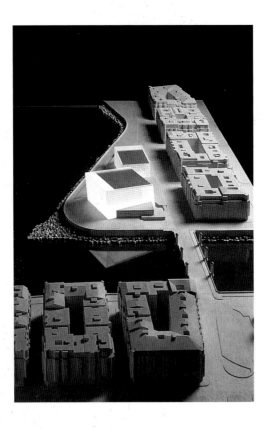

Rafael Moneo is probably the internationally best known living Spanish architect. As stated in the introduction, Moneo's architecture helps build the city. The contextualization of his works determines their character. Together with his respect for the context, his skilful use of traditional materials, especially brick, and his complete understanding of a modern, simple architecture have allowed him to design some of the recent Spanish architectural masterpieces.

In this publication, which presents three of his most recent (and still under construction) projects, Moneo is to be understood both as a teacher of many of the architects included here, and as a very active and creative practicing architect. Now in his early fifties, Moneo is probably in the heyday of his professional career, and his architecture continues to be as innovative and imaginative, as well as inspirational to other architects, as it has always been.

Like giant rocks by the mouth of the Urumea river, two cubical volumes contain the auditorium and conference center. The supporting platform, which accommodates the rest of the program's miscellaneous functions, raises both geometrical figures to provide them with an enhanced view of the seascape. The new structures violate the urban grid to become perfectly integrated with the landscape where they stand.

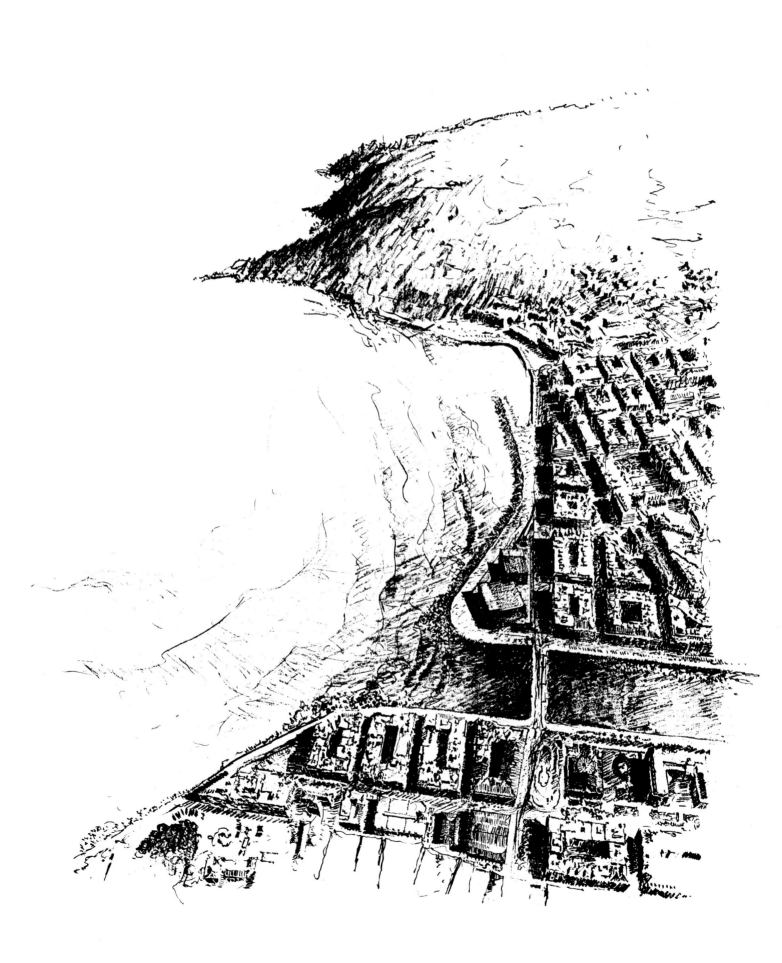

Perspective, from the sea

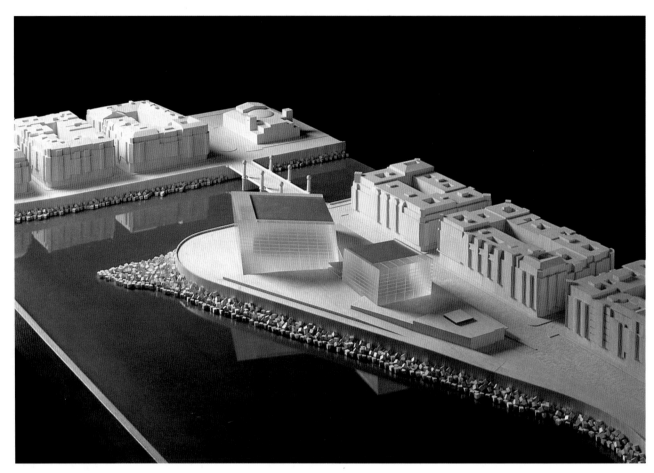

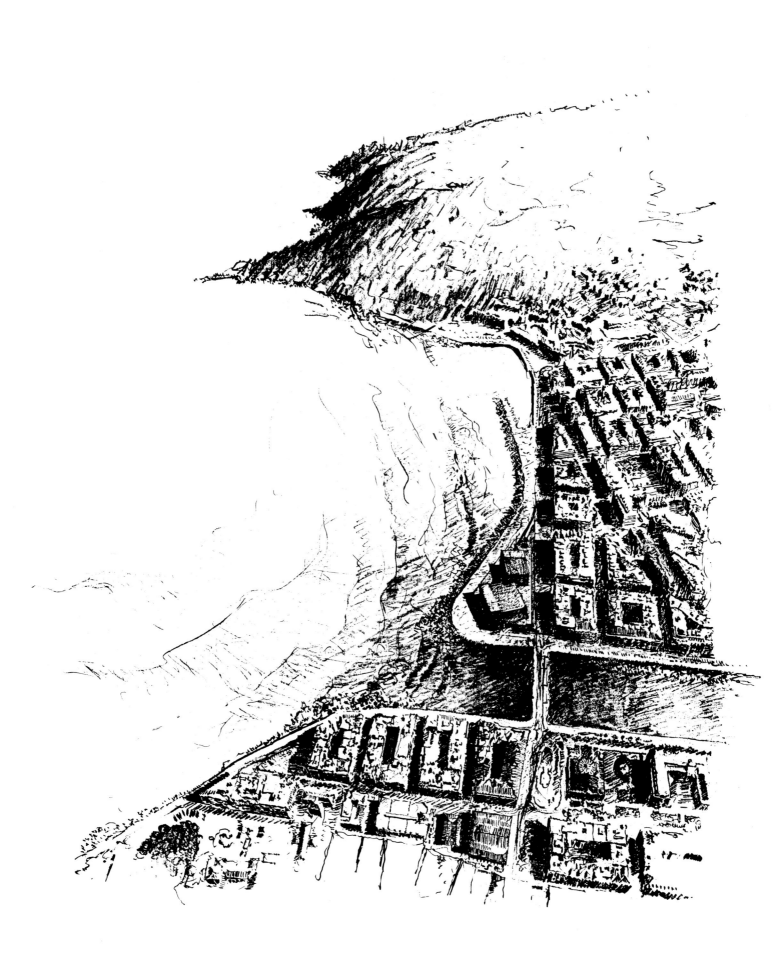

Perspective, from the sea

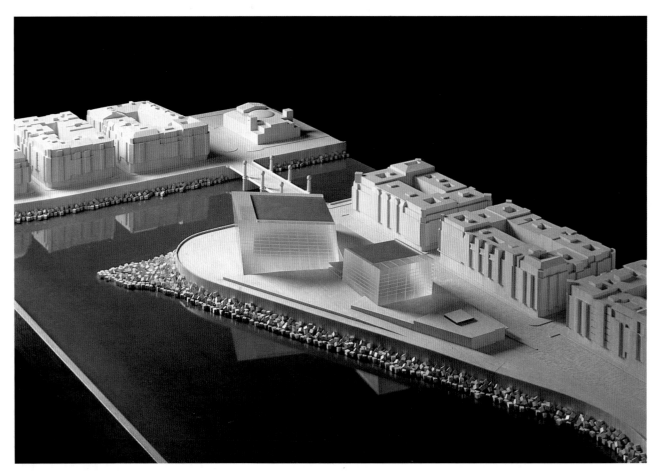

Perspective, from the street

RAFAEL MONEO   175

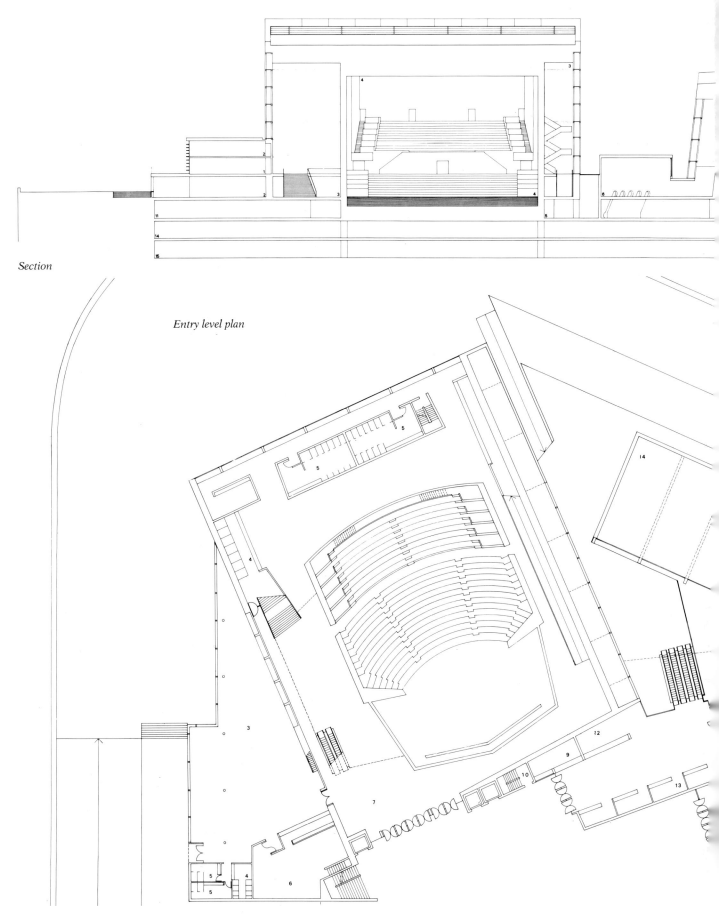

Section

Entry level plan

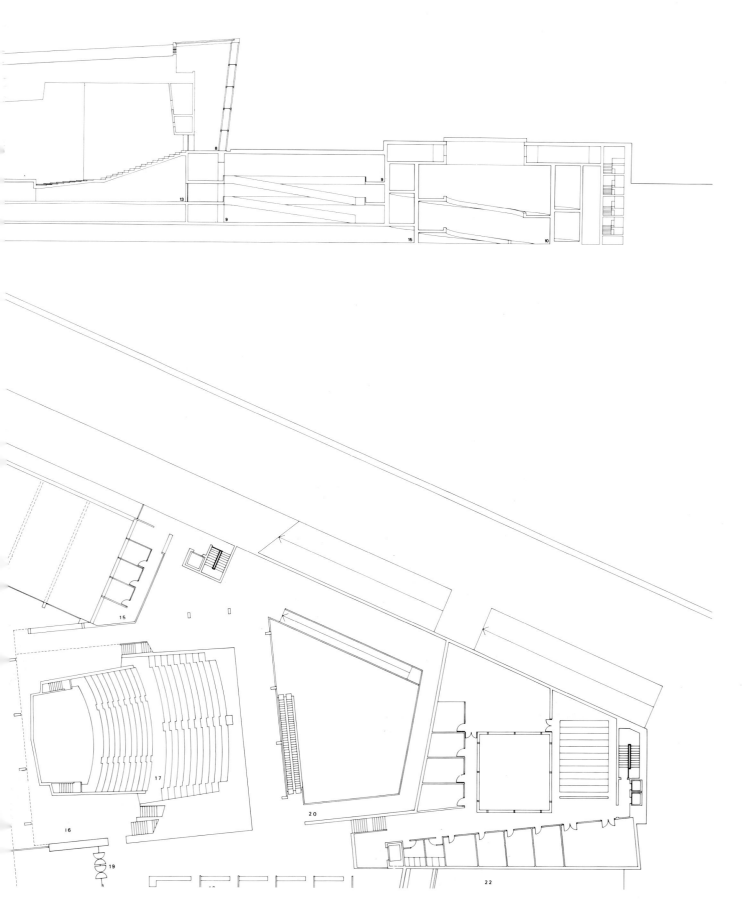

Miró Foundation • Palma de Mallorca • 1989–91

The building will host both temporary exhibitions of visiting art collections and the foundation's own permanent collection. A documentation and study center for those doing research on Miró has also been planned.

The new building is located next to the studio Josep Lluis Sert designed for the artist, and has been influenced by the sloped topography of the area, as well as by the size and character of the surrounding buildings. A starlike floor plan was chosen, allowing for differentiated areas and exhibition spaces for the future activities of the foundation.

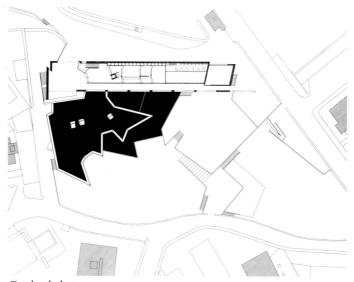

Top level plan

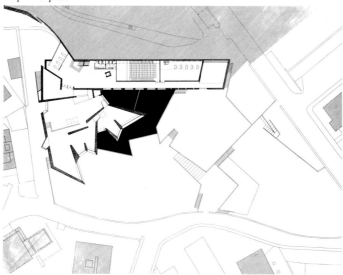

Middle level plan

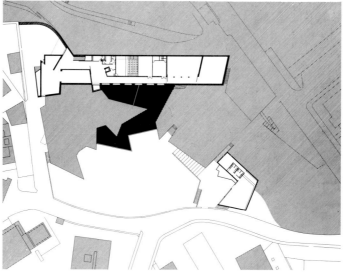

Lower level plan

Section

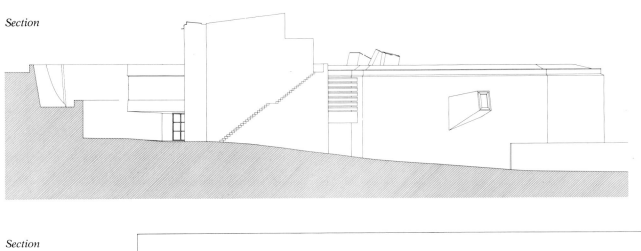

Section

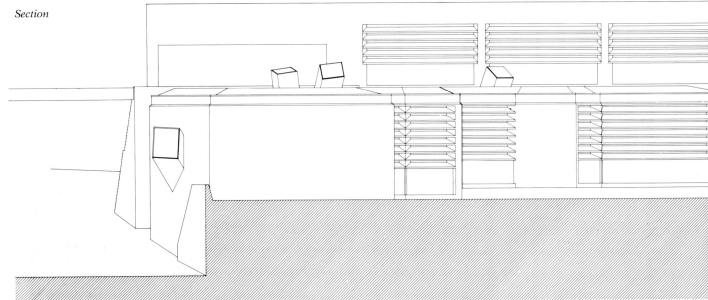

Section

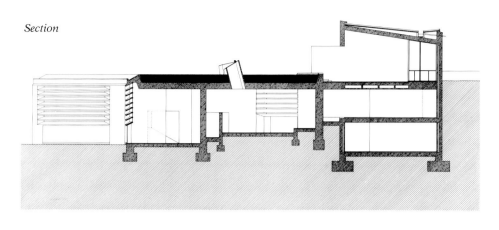

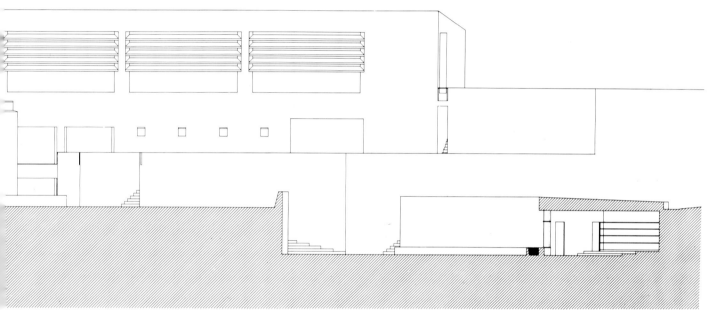

Auditorium • Barcelona • 1988-
(with Maria Fraile)

Located in a suburban area of Barcelona that has been increasingly absorbed by the city, adjacent to the new Catalan National Theater by Ricardo Bofill, and also near the new Olympic Village residential area and a recently opened public square, the new auditorium will continue the radical transformation of this urban zone.

The building is organized around a central covered patio which serves as the entrance hall, reception area, and ticket offices.

The complex functional program required the construction of two concert halls; the main auditorium plus a smaller one to host the chamber music concerts. The program also incorporates several other services, such as a library, a cafeteria, a bar, locker rooms, practice rooms for musicians, storage areas, dressing rooms, and the new location for the Music Museum of Barcelona. A crucial part of Barcelona's comprehensive urban remodeling, Moneo's auditorium is scheduled for completion by the end of 1992.

Elevations

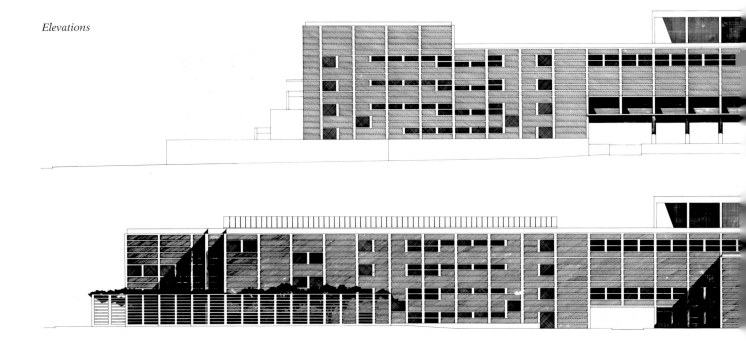

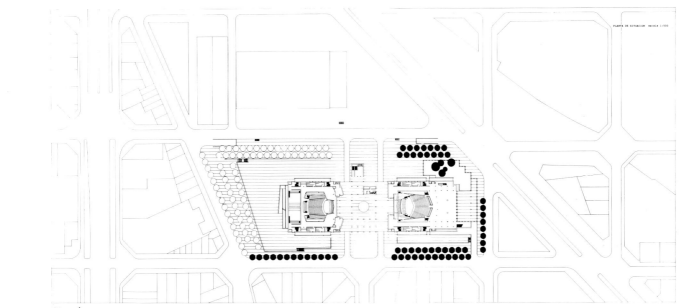

Site plan

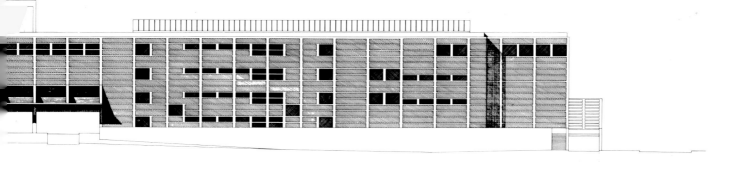

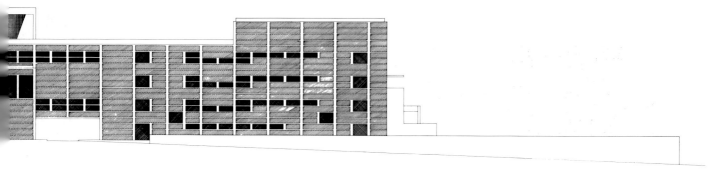

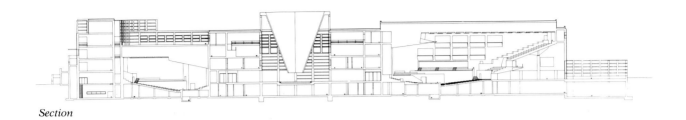

Section

Lower level plan

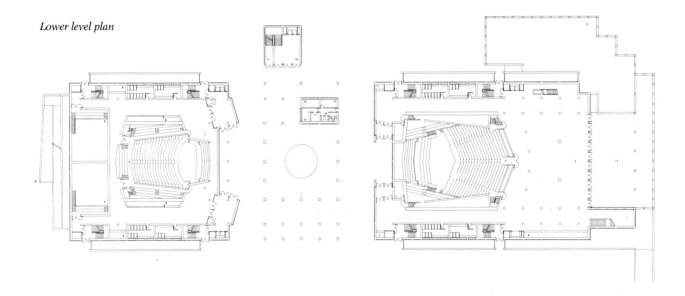

First floor plan

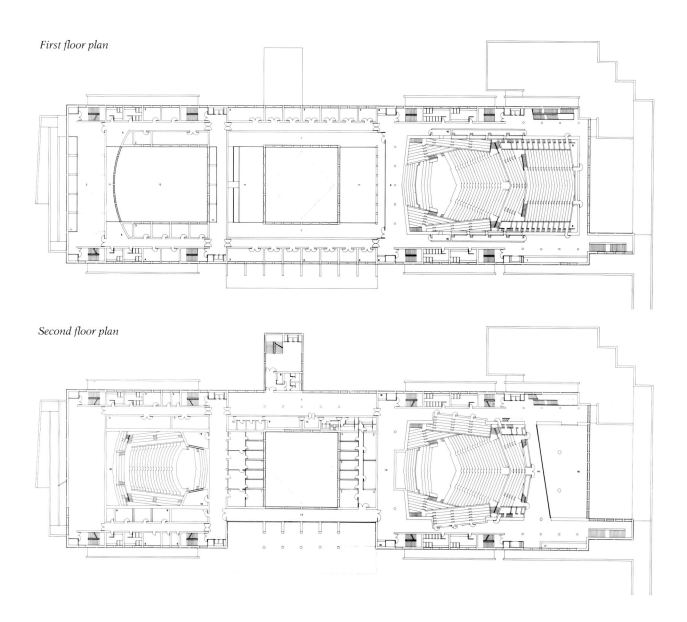

Second floor plan

CESAR PORTELA

Aquarium · Villagarcía de Arousa · Pontevedra · 1987

To this Galician architect, architecture equals artifice and is therefore opposed to nature. For him, good architecture is the resulting dialogue of a program and a place, a stage where life takes place.

Influenced by art history and nature, the strongest reference in his work is taken from the indigenous Galician rural house, the *pazo*, as well as from traditional materials and construction methods of the area. His response to the Modern Movement has been to absorb its principles and to apply them to his own cultural and architectural tradition. César Portela's architecture is the construction required by men respectfully adapted to nature. What remains to be seen is how accurate the adaptation would be outside his natural and cultural surroundings.

The coast of Galicia represents a permanent dialogue between land and ocean resulting in the many estuaries that characterize the area.

The aquarium designed by Portela poetically enters the ocean. Its location contrasts with the reinforced concrete structure that gives the building its solid, monolithic shape. Echoes of the *horreo*, a traditional Galician building type, respect for traditional forms, the use of regional materials, and integration with the landscape—Portela's most defining characteristics—are well represented in this project.

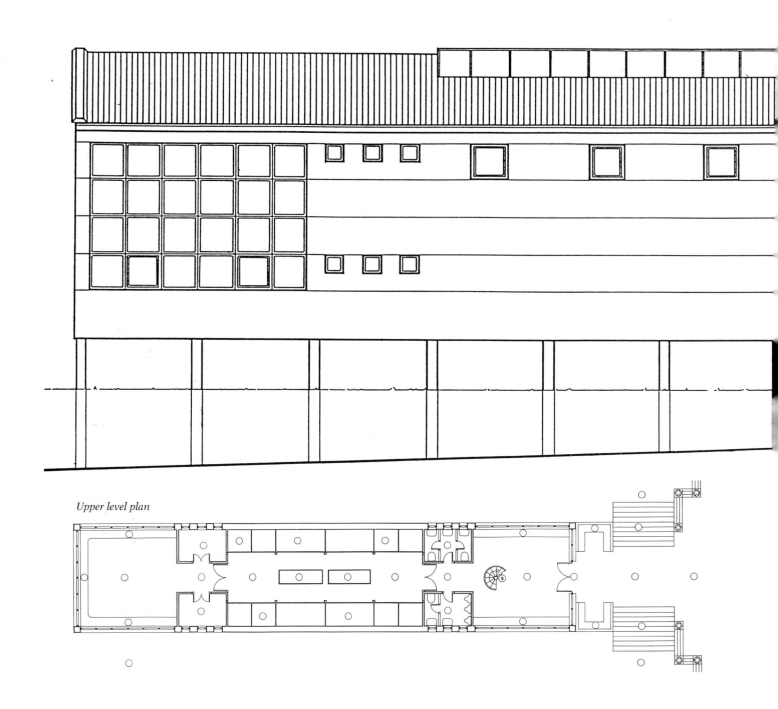

Upper level plan

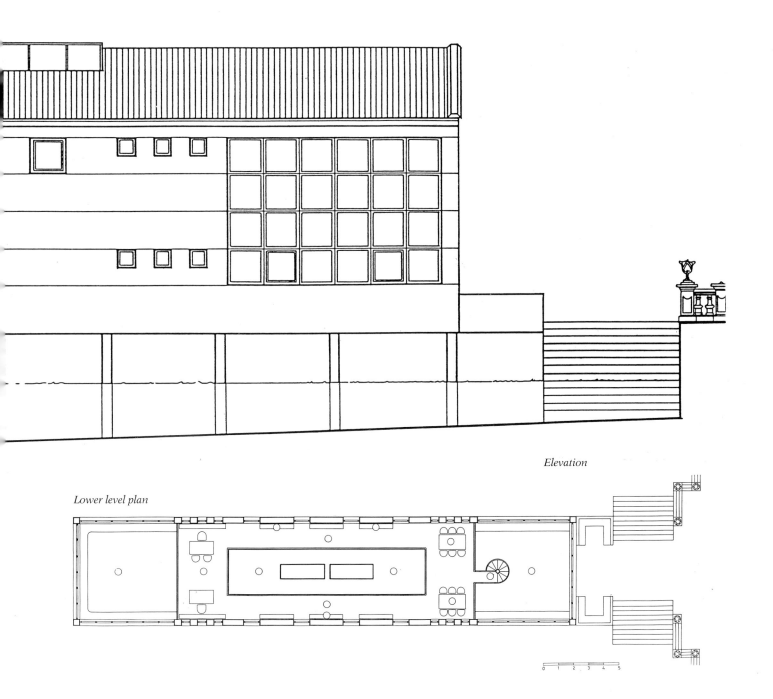

Elevation

Lower level plan

Pino House · Vilaxoan · Rías de Arousa · Pontevedra · 1989

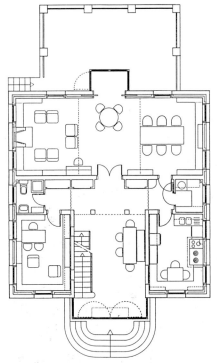

Lower level plan

This single family house owes its shape to the long and deep plot of land where it is located. The supporting structure rests on two gray granite walls, a very commonly used material in the area, while the interior spaces all open to the three-story glass section that, facing south, constitutes the warmest area in the house.

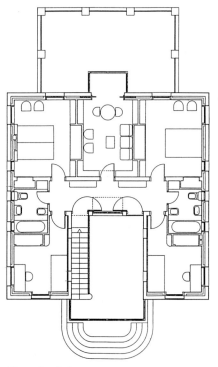

Upper level plan

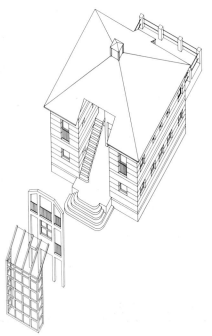

Exploded axonometric of entry

Cultural Center · Cangas · Pontevedra · 1989

The building hosts exhibitions, lectures, and courses, acting as a cultural center at the seaside village of Cangas. Strategically located on the coast, the con-struction can be seen from the city across the estuary. Its architectural typology refers back to the traditional construction of this region, the *horreo*. The building's interior layout is organized around a central three-story-high patio.

Section 1-1

Section 2-2

Ground floor plan

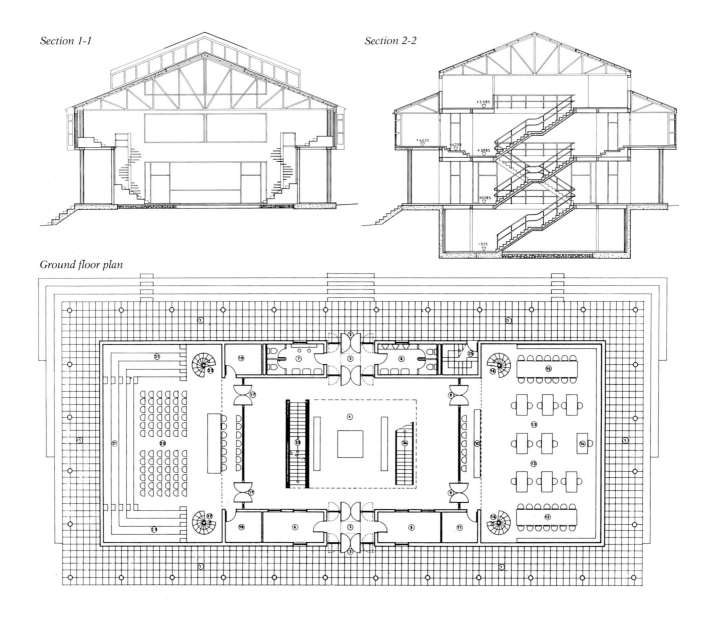

JOSE LUIS SOLANS/ PILAR BRIALES/RICARDO DEL AMO

Angela Navarro Beauty Center • Madrid • 1990

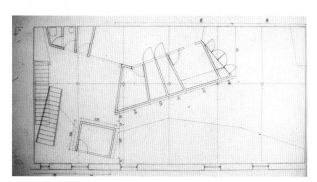

Lower level plan

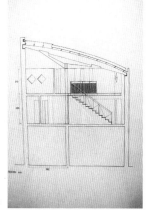

Section

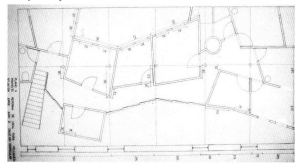

Entry level plan

José Luis Solans and Pilar Briales opened their own architecture studio in 1977. Ricardo del Amo joined the partnership in 1984. A Minorcan native, he had designed many residential projects built on the island. In 1983, the three started working for the Hachuel family in what was to be the first of a series of projects the studio was able to design with almost complete freedom. In the Hachuel house, they were able to produce a comprehensive architecture that encompassed every construction detail, the furniture, and the landscape. Some of their smaller projects, like the Angela Navarro Beauty Center and the Antonio de Amberes Foundation, illustrate their ability to create the new from the old, using intuition, plastic taste, and creativity to redefine new spatial layouts within an existing structure. Acknowledging debts to Alvar Aalto and Mies van der Rohe, and therefore recognizing the influence that the Modern Movement has had on their work, Solans, Briales and del Amo are among the most creative and innovative architects to be found in Spain. Singularly original in their breaking up of space and use of industrial materials, their architecture is contemporarily modern, for it acknowledges International Style references while employing current technology and materials.

The commission was to transform a 1910 building into a beauty center. The new treelike supporting structure, which was left exposed, allowed for several two-story spaces. The red structure, formed by five supporting columns, also permitted the functions to be organized according to a zigzag-like floor plan. This design allowed for the largest possible number of cubicles in the upper floor.

Madrid Pavilion • Expo 92 • Seville • 1989

The architects were commissioned to design a pavilion that would represent the city of Madrid at the 1992 World Expo in Seville. It needed to be an emblematic building, open and flexible enough to accommodate the many different activities that are to take place there. A reticulate, cubic composition, made of perfect smaller cubes, was chosen as the visible structure of the pavilion, with star-shaped light reflectors in the four facades.

Circulation around the six-story building is organized by means of elevators, stairs, and ramps, that provide access to the various services provided by the pavilion: auditorium, press conference room, exhibition hall, information center, and restaurants.

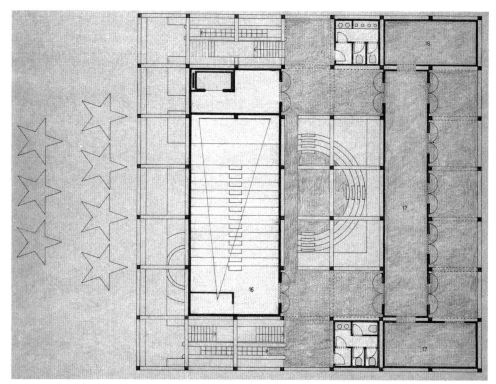

Fifth floor plan

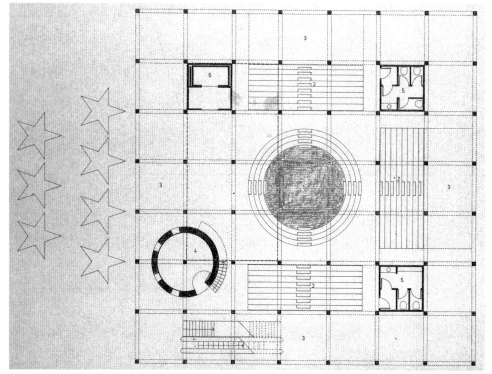

Ground floor plan

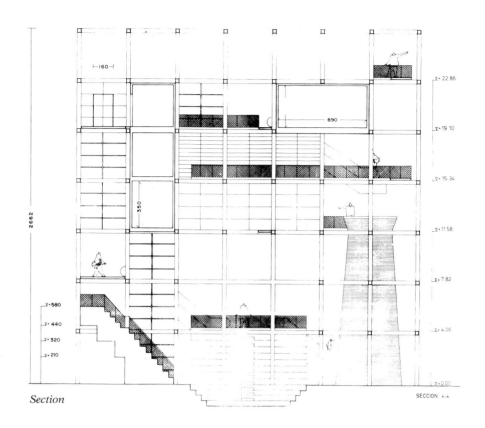

Section

SECCION 4-4

Hachuel House • Puerta del Hierro • Madrid • 1990

The house is the result of a seven-year period of changes in its design and interior organization, due to the shifting demands of the client. The construction had to be undertaken while the owners were living in the house. Having completed the first commission to enlarge the house, the architects added a new library and, as the clients' art collection grew, the exhibition space in the house had to be adapted and restructured. As a result, some of the recently added elements, floating pavilions, can be moved around easily, varying the interior organization and exterior appearance of the house.

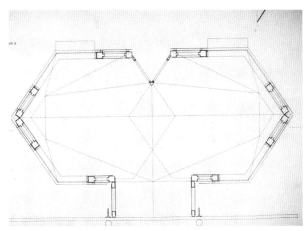

Hexagonal pavilion plan

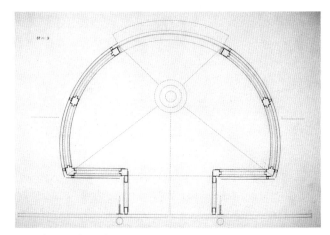

Circular pavilion plan

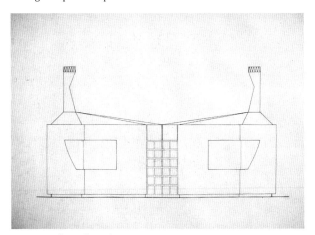

Hexagonal pavilion elevation

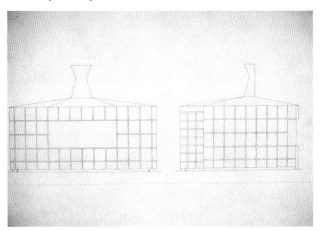

Circular pavilion elevation

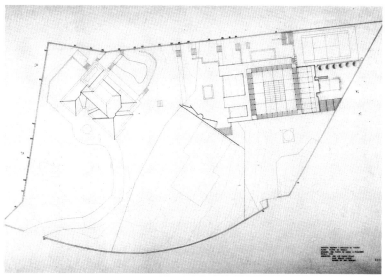

Site plan

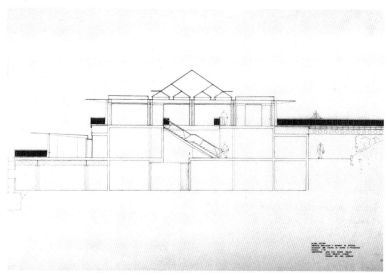

Section

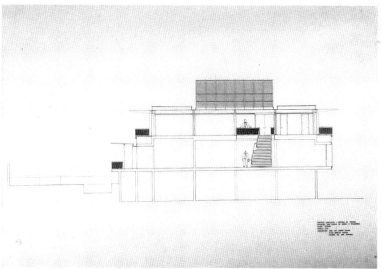

Section

PEP ZAZURCA

Concepción School • Barcelona • 1991 (with Mariona Muxart)

Axonometric, corner detail

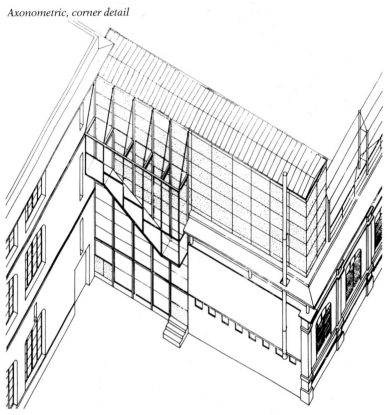

Zazurca's architecture is about manipulation, alteration, and the transformation of old buildings. Most of the time, his work is more difficult, complex, and expensive than creating a new building. Reuse of some of the original parts, reorganization of the old construction, rather than wrapping the existing building, is his purpose. He first became popular through the remodeling of an early bourgeois house. The original structure, of a Catalan 'modernist' (Art Nouveau) style and of little architectural value, had already been transformed into a bar, although the architec-

tural intervention of the previous firm had been limited to redesigning the interior architecture. Zazurca´s transformation included changes in the access and circulation areas inside and outside the building, as well as changes in style and ornament, juxtaposing Secessionist and Scarpa-esque influences with the existing Art Nouveau.

In the three recent projects presented here, the conditions are quite similar. Zazurca starts with a building of little architectural interest in which he is given almost complete freedom to reconstruct it and adapt it to its new

use. He reduces the original structure to remains, scraps, which, through new juxtapositions, establish architectural dialogues, confrontations, and superpositions. The aim is to meld old and new into a new architectonic order that combines both, using the original parts and traces, not as references, but as motifs of intervention. In his work, these interventions are very strong; windows become doors, doors may also become windows, and new accesses and functions are created.

In his juxtaposition of elements, Zazurca's international references reach as far as Los

Angeles, to the architecture of Frank Gehry and the Morphosis studio, with their use of industrial materials and layout of spaces. Although Zazurca's studio constantly combines past references with new elements, trying to improve what already exists, he cannot be included in the postmodernist group, for he does not recreate past styles and traditions. Nor can he be called a neomodern, for he does not attack one's perception of architecture with broken angularities. With a noticeable debt to the Catalan architect Josep Coderch, Zazurca's work tries to make the

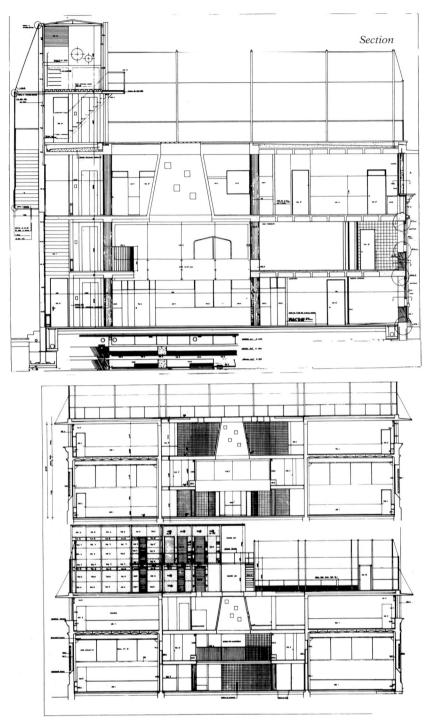

Section

Section

most of what there is, searching for references and ideas not only in architecture but also in contemporary art.

For historical reasons, the Barcelona city council and the Catalonian government decided to retain some parts of the existing school building, and to extend it. The central part of the old structure was emptied and transformed into a new core, lit by natural light, around which the school classrooms were to be organized. The upper floor was added to increase the building's height and all floors were connected by a staircase that reveals the building's section. The sports area and locker rooms were placed on the roof.

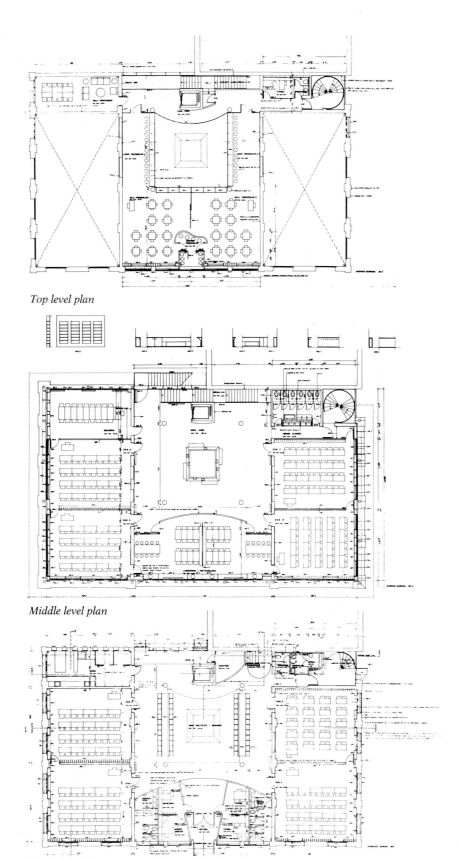

Top level plan

Middle level plan

Lower level plan

F. Turro Office Building • Barcelona • 1991
(with Mar Ruiz and Gabriel Coll)

The existing structure, a single family house built in 1925, has been transformed into an office building through three major changes: the modification of the facades with new openings; the transformation of the interior spaces through the replacement of some of the structural elements by new ones, obtaining both larger working spaces and better connections among them. Lastly, new glass and metal elements were designed to complement the old materials.

North elevation

Third floor plan

Second floor plan

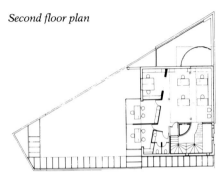

Ground floor plan

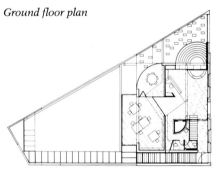

Basement plan

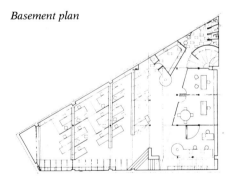

Sub-basement plan

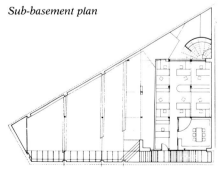

Z House • Barcelona • 1991 (with Gabriel Coll)

This single family house has been completely transformed. A new column structure, placed very close to the façade, allows for great freedom when locating the house's interior partitions and creating new openings. On the exterior, another new, thin steel structure has been erected opposing the existing facades, recomposing the building, and breaking away at the same time from the existing house. The old façade is therefore placed, as in a sandwich, between the new metal structure and the new interior columns. The glass staircase organizes the interior space which has been completely designed by the architects (all furniture included) taking Donald Judd, sailing, and Philippe Starck as their main references.

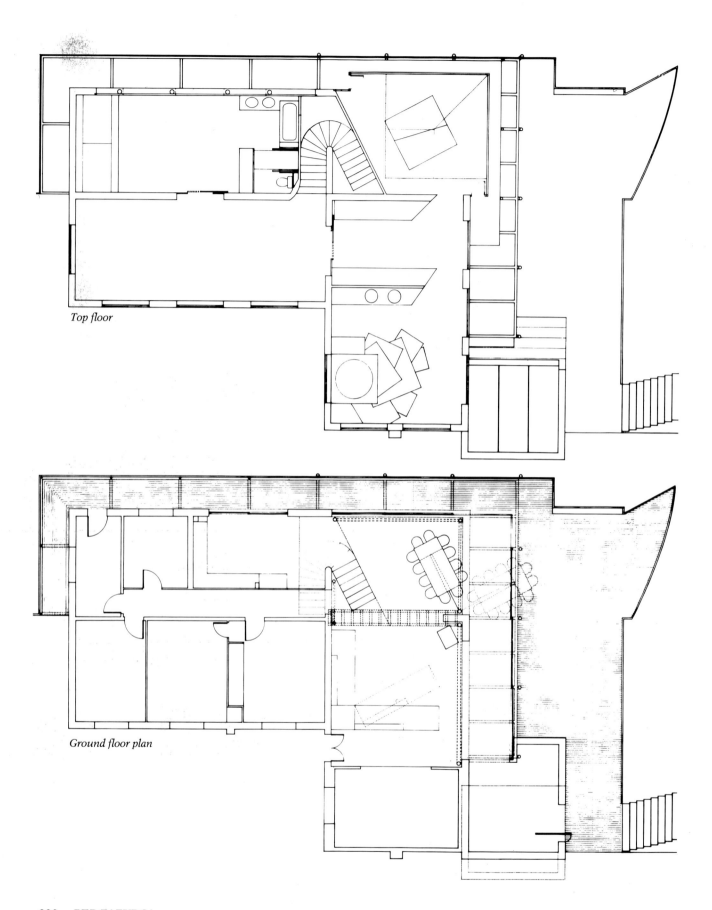

Top floor

Ground floor plan

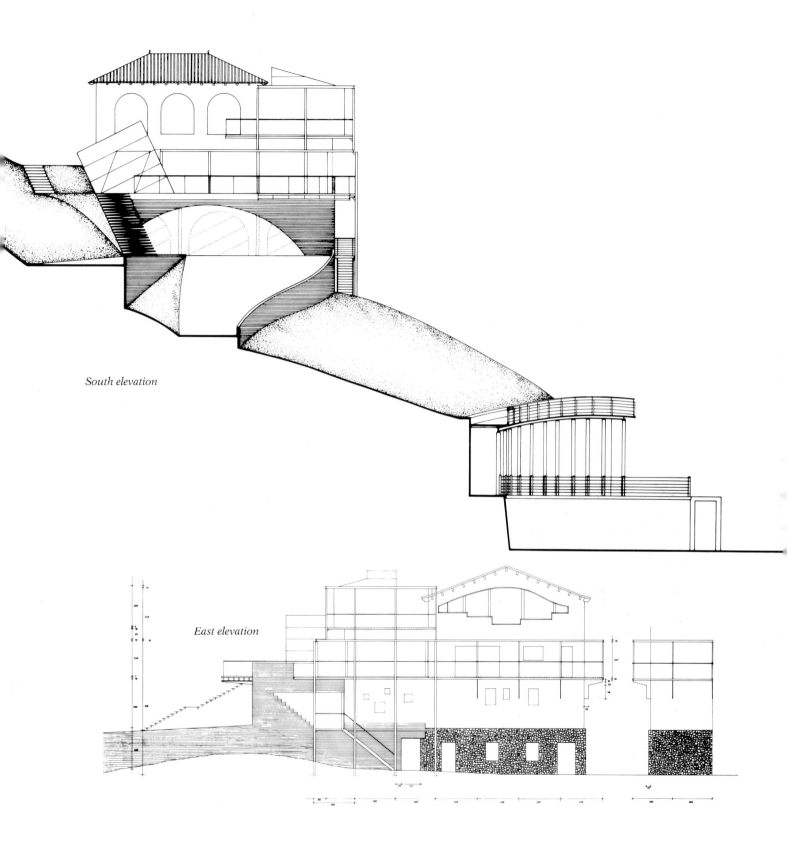

South elevation

East elevation

222   PEP ZAZURCA